BOSTON Herald

BOSTON RED SOX

2004 WORLD SERIES CHAMPIONS

SP
SPORTS
PUBLISHING
L.L.C.

www.SportsPublishingLLC.com

PRESIDENT AND PUBLISHER: Patrick J. Purcell
EDITORIAL DIRECTOR: Kenneth A. Chandler
MANAGING EDITOR: Kevin R. Convey
EXECUTIVE SPORTS EDITOR: Mark Torpey
DIRECTOR OF PHOTOGRAPHY: Jim Mahoney
VICE PRESIDENT/PROMOTION: Gwen Gage
CHIEF LIBRARIAN: John Cronin

PUBLISHERS: Peter L. Bannon and Joseph J. Bannon Sr.
SENIOR MANAGING EDITOR: Susan M. Moyer
ACQUISITIONS EDITOR: Joseph J. Bannon Jr.
COORDINATING EDITOR: Noah Adams Amstadter
DEVELOPMENTAL EDITORS: Elisa Bock Laird and Dean Miller
ART DIRECTOR: K. Jeffrey Higgerson
BOOK DESIGN: Jennifer L. Polson
DUST JACKET DESIGN: Dustin Hubbart
BOOK LAYOUT: Kathryn R. Holleman and Jim Henehan
IMAGING: K. Jeffrey Higgerson, Dustin Hubbart and Kenneth J. O'Brien
PHOTO EDITOR: Erin Linden-Levy
VICE PRESIDENT OF SALES AND MARKETING: Kevin King
MEDIA AND PROMOTIONS MANAGERS: Nick Obradovich (regional),
Randy Fouts (national), Maurey Williamson (print)

Front cover photo by Matt Stone/Boston Herald
Back cover photo by Tara Bricking/Boston Herald

ISBN: 1-59670-029-7 (softcover edition)
1-59670-028-9 (hardcover edition)

Printed in the United States

Sports Publishing L.L.C.
804 North Neil Street
Champaign, IL 61820

Phone: 1-877-424-2665
Fax: 217-363-2073
Web site: www.SportsPublishingLLC.com

CONTENTS

Tara Bricking/Boston Herald

David Goldman/Boston Herald

Stuart Cahill/Boston Herald

NEWSPAPER CREDITS

The entire staff of the *Boston Herald* photography department contributed to the coverage
of the Boston Red Sox' 2004 season, which culminated in a World Series victory.
We gratefully acknowledge the efforts of staff photographers:

Michael Adaskaveg
Tara Bricking
Stuart Cahill
Renee DeKona
Robert Eng
Michael Fein
Ted Fitzgerald
Mark Garfinkel
David Goldman
Jon Hill
Nancy Lane
Douglas McFadd
Faith Ninivaggi
Angela Rowlings
Michael Seamans
Matt Stone
Matthew West
Patrick Whittemore
John Wilcox

Jim Mahoney, Director of Photography
Ted Ancher, Assistant Director
Arthur Pollock, Assistant Director
John Landers, Night Picture Editor

SPRING TRAINING

Nomar and Trot are out until May. A-Rod is with the Yankees. Pedro is throwing a John Burkett fastball. The new closer has been awful. And none of the November free agents has agreed to a contract extension.

Considering what has happened this spring, it would be natural to assume that the Red Sox' final few days in the Sunshine State would have been dark and gloomy. But when they departed following a 4-3 win over the Minnesota Twins at Hammond Stadium, it was clear optimism still abounds.

"This is still the best team out there," center fielder Johnny Damon said. "It's going to be tougher because of the injuries, but we've got pretty good players filling in."

Thanks to the offseason bolstering of the bench, no one is panicking about the string of misfortune that struck over the past seven weeks. General manager Theo Epstein took advantage of ownership's approval to bump the payroll up to $130 million and re-signed Gabe Kapler, David McCarty, Alan Embree and Mike Timlin, acquired Curt Schilling and Mark Bellhorn, and signed free agents Ellis Burks, Pokey Reese and Brian Daubach. The series of moves left the Sox prepared to handle the glut of injuries that put them to the test before the season's first pitch.

"I feel every bit as good about this team's chances of going all the way as the day I came here, if not better," Schilling said.

Even so, the tests of Boston's mettle have been constant:

A-Rod goes south

The first sign that nothing was going to come easy occurred just before the opening of camp, when the New York Yankees stunned the sports world by acquiring Alex Rodriguez from the Texas Rangers. Boston made a relentless effort to deal for the reigning American League MVP in December but was forced to give up when the Players Association refused to OK the financial restructuring of his enormous contract.

Stars not aligned

Sox management had contracts on its collective mind due to the impending free agency of Nomar Garciaparra, Pedro Martinez, Derek Lowe and Jason Varitek. Ownership acknowledged it would like to re-sign at least one of the four before breaking camp, but that wasn't accomplished despite quiet negotiations with each. None of the four was happy with the offers received, and as it stands today, all are destined to file for free agency after the World Series.

It hurts so bad

Last year, only one position player (Jeremy Giambi) landed on the disabled list.

This season, two starters are already on it. Garciaparra had his feelings hurt by the Sox' attempts to replace him with A-Rod, and his Achilles' tendon was hurt when he was struck by a line drive in batting practice on March 5. The two-time batting champion was limited to eight Grapefruit League at-bats, and he learned he would be sidelined for at least three weeks.

ABOVE: Sox David Ortiz has some fun pointing out a teammate during spring training practice. (Matthew West/Boston Herald)

That was actually a better diagnosis than received by Trot Nixon, who was barely able to get on the field due to a bulging disc in his back. The right fielder, who hit .306 with 24 home runs last season, is currently rehabbing at a Miami spine clinic and isn't likely to return until May.

Pedro not in fast lane

Martinez, meanwhile, insisted throughout the spring that he felt stronger than he had since 1997, but it didn't show on the radar guns. His fastball, which was routinely in the 93-96 mph range last season, peaked at 91 in his final three starts. Publicly, the team said it isn't concerned and professed faith that Martinez would be able to step it up on Sunday at Camden Yards.

That's all, Foulke?

Closer Keith Foulke was lit up in Florida, but manager Terry Francona, who was on his coaching staff in Oakland last season, said it's an annual occurrence. Even so, a 13.50 ERA and .375 opponents batting average did little to instill confidence in those who haven't seen him on a regular basis.

News isn't all bad

There were, of course, plenty of encouraging signs. Schilling showed that 2003 injuries had no lasting impact and he remained overpowering. Manny Ramirez displayed a cheerful disposition, despite nearly being traded for A-Rod, while David Ortiz showed he's ready to add to his breakout season. Kapler, who will

ABOVE: Sox pitcher Alan Embree fires from the mound as palm trees line the background. (Matthew West/Boston Herald)

open the season in right field, provided the spring's biggest surprise by moving to third base for the first time as a pro and handling the hot corner like a Gold Glove winner.

"I feel good about everything, I really do," Francona said. "Now it's time to play, regardless of who's hurt or whatever.

"Our job is to win. We have to find a way to be one run better. Nothing else matters."

RIGHT: Sox shortstop Nomar Garciaparra jokes with new skipper Terry Francona during spring training. The Sox are optimistic going into the regular season despite some offseason setbacks. (Matthew West/Boston Herald)

" I feel every bit as good about this team's chances of going all the way as the day I came here, if not better. "

—Curt Schilling

TERRY FRANCONA

BY MICHAEL SILVERMAN

He will pull out of his driveway near Philadelphia on Feb. 15, the day before the Red Sox' equipment truck leaves Fenway Park, so there is not much preventing Terry Francona from getting beat by anything in his drive to Fort Myers.

Heading south on I-95, the Red Sox' new skipper will not be heading for parts unknown. He will enter his rookie season as the Red Sox' skipper as prepared as a manager possibly could be, a map of the preseason already laid out in his mind. Even finding City of Palms Park will not be an issue, as Francona already checked it out over the winter holidays.

Preparation is key to Francona's modus operandi, and while he is not using a pen yet to figure out a game plan and a starting nine for the 2004 season, he has already sharpened his pencil many times.

By the middle of January, he and bench coach Brad Mills had mapped out every day of spring training to the point where Francona knows which batch of hitters he is throwing batting practice to on the first day of camp. This off-season, Francona has been spending time in the Red Sox front offices, getting to know staff, poring over written analyses of Red Sox players and trying to contact all the members of the 40-man roster and many minor-leaguers as well.

"I've not actually talked to every single player, but it's been pretty darn close," said Francona last week. "I'll pick four or five guys every night and call them, or leave some voicemail. I'm just excited to meet all of them and getting to know them."

He and Pedro Martinez bumped into each other in the Red Sox' clubhouse a couple of weeks ago, he's been in touch with Nomar Garciaparra and Curt Schilling a few times, plus he and David Ortiz finally connected. As for Manny Ramirez, Francona said, "I have left him a lot of messages and talked to a lot of his family members. Manny's aware that I've called, and that's good enough for me."

There are not many key roster spots to be won this spring training, outside of some utility player jobs. Kevin Millar is still the first baseman, Ortiz is the DH, and Pokey Reese is the second baseman with Mark Bellhorn getting a turn there now and then as well. Francona seems particularly excited about the upside of pitchers Ramiro Mendoza and Bronson Arroyo.

Mendoza, whose 2003 season was a lost one, no longer has any physical restraints and will hopefully be used as he was for the Yankees, as both a swing-man and late-inning reliever.

And Arroyo, said Francona, "is going to be a real interesting wild card. He caught everyone's attention last year, and it's going to be real interesting where he goes with it."

So Francona is heading south with an uncluttered and open mind.

"I don't want any surprises, only the good kind," he said. "I want to enjoy my drive, the peace and quiet. Although I'm sure 10 hours into it, I'll be wondering, `What was I thinking?'"

SOX DUST OFF YANKS

BY JEFF HORRIGAN, BOSTON HERALD

With Grady Little literally smiling upon them from above, the Red Sox found out what can happen when Pedro Martinez is pulled out of a game with a lead after seven innings at Yankee Stadium.

Martinez, pitching in the Bronx for the first time since failing to hold a three-run lead in the eighth inning of Game 7 of the 2003 American League Championship Series, was lifted by new manager Terry Francona after seven dominating frames. Francona handed the ball to Scott Williamson, who wrapped up a 2-0 win over the New York Yankees with two perfect innings.

The combined four-hitter gave the Sox a three-game series sweep and allowed them to improve to 6-1 against their rivals this season. The series sweep of New York was the Red Sox' first since Sept. 10-12, 1999, also at Yankee Stadium, and it marked the first time since 1988 that the Sox took the first two series of a season from the Yankees.

"Of course we're happy to sweep," center fielder Johnny Damon said. "I just wish we could go back to last year and make these games count."

Martinez allowed four hits, while striking out seven batters.

Fans in the front row of the top deck of Yankee Stadium, just above the visitors dugout, attached photos of a smiling Little to the facade

	1	2	3		4	5	6		7	8	9		R	H	E
Boston	0	0	0		2	0	0		0	0	0		2	4	0
NY Yankees	0	0	0		0	0	0		0	0	0		0	4	2

Boston	AB	R	H	RBI
Damon, CF	3	0	0	0
Bellhorn, 3B	3	1	0	0
Ortiz, DH	4	0	2	0
Ramirez, LF	3	1	2	2
Millar, RF	3	0	0	0
Kapler, RF	0	0	0	0
Varitek, C	4	0	0	0
McCarty, 1B	3	0	0	0
Crespo, 2B	4	0	0	0
Reese, SS	4	0	0	0
Totals	31	2	4	2

NY Yankees	AB	R	H	RBI
Jeter, SS	4	0	0	0
Williams, CF	4	0	0	0
Rodriguez, 3B	4	0	2	0
Giambi, 1B	4	0	0	0
Sheffield, RF	4	0	1	0
Posada, C	2	0	0	0
Matsui, LF	3	0	0	0
Sierra, R., DH	3	0	1	0
Wilson, 2B	2	0	0	0
Lee, PH	1	0	0	0
Cairo, 2B	0	0	0	0
Totals	31	0	4	0

2B: Ortiz,R. Sierra, Rodriguez; HR: Ramirez (5); SB: Rodriguez; E: Posada, Jeter.

Boston	IP	H	R	ER	BB	SO
Martinez, P (W, 3-1)	7.0	4	0	0	1	7
Williamson (S, 1)	2.0	0	0	0	0	2

NY Yankees	IP	H	R	ER	BB	SO
Vazquez (L, 2-2)	6.0	4	2	2	1	8
Quantrill	1.0	0	0	0	0	1
White	0.2	0	0	0	1	0
Gordon	0.1	0	0	0	1	1
Rivera	1.0	0	0	0	1	1

WP: Gordon; HBP: Millar (by Vazquez); T: 2:48; Att: 55,338.

OPPOSITE: Sox Kevin Millar congratulates Manny Ramirez after his two-run homer in the fourth. That run sealed the win and the sweep of the Yankees at home. (Tara Bricking/Boston Herald)

"Of course we're happy to sweep. I just wish we could go back to last year and make these games count."

—Johnny Damon

ABOVE: Sox pitcher Pedro Martinez, pitching for the first time in Yankee Stadium since failing to hold a three-run lead in Game 7 of the 2003 ALCS, allowed the Yankees only four hits and struck out seven batters. (Tara Bricking/Boston Herald)

about the character of this team. We haven't clicked all the way through offensively, but we will. For now, we're just getting 'Ws' and that's what it's all about."

Williamson, who saved all three Red Sox wins in the ALCS, said last October's disappointment never entered his mind.

"I don't think about last year," Williamson said. "I don't think, 'What if we did this or that, things would be different.' These are totally different circumstances. The only thing that's the same is our uniforms. What happened is over and hopefully things will be different now and this team WILL go to a World Series and win a World Series. I don't see why we can't."

After becoming the first team ever (or at least since it started getting tracked in 1974) to go 0-for-19 at the plate with

each time a Red Sox batter struck out. The attempt to distract the Sox failed miserably, as it was the Yankees who fell apart for the third consecutive game.

"We all remember Game 7, but this is a new year," right fielder Kevin Millar said. "We went out and played a good series and that tells you

runners in scoring position and still find a way to win in the second game of the series, the Sox went 1-for-4 on such occasions. Manny Ramirez poked a base hit to center field after David Ortiz reached on a double in the sixth inning, but both runners ended up stranded.

By that point, however, the Red Sox already had enough runs thanks to Ramirez' two-run homer off Yankees starting pitcher Javier Vazquez in the fifth. On an 0-2 count, Ramirez crushed a hanging curveball over Monument Park in left-center field and into the visitors' bullpen. The blast, which traveled approximately 450 feet, was Ramirez' fifth of the season and 352nd of his career, tying him with teammate Ellis Burks for 68th on the all-time list.

"Only one guy on this team hit for us this weekend and that was Manny," Damon said. "Wait until the rest of us join the hit parade."

Martinez and Williamson made the lead stand. Martinez, who buckled batters with a sharp curveball, allowed four runners to advance into scoring position but held the Yankees hitless in six at-bats under such circumstances.

"You have to talk about the whole team," Martinez said in a statement issued by the team. "They never gave up. They played hard. It was up to me to step up and give them a chance to win."

BELOW: Mike Sage of Clifton, New Jersey, and Bonnie Stone of Chickopee, Massachusetts, cheer for the Sox after they completed a three-game sweep of the Yankees at Yankee Stadium. (Tara Bricking/Boston Herald)

P
45

PEDRO MARTINEZ

BY TONY MASSAROTTI

This time, when he walked off the mound at the conclusion of the seventh inning, there were no doubts he was done. His manager walked the length of the dugout and shook his hand. His pitching coach patted him on the knee. He got up from his seat and hugged teammate David Ortiz then disappeared with a smile down the runway to the clubhouse.

And after the game, when he spoke with Spanish reporters, he acknowledged what we have all known for some time.

"I'm not the pitcher who will throw 97 [mph] all the time," Pedro Martinez said following a 2-0 Red Sox victory against the Yankees that completed a sweep in the Bronx. "I'm a more mature pitcher. I pitch to my strengths. If I pitch to my strengths, velocity isn't important. I think I can be consistently 93, 92, 91. If you do that, then velocity is just a number."

At this point, his numbers look like this: A 3-1 record, a 3.03 ERA and 28 strikeouts in 32 2/3 innings. Opponents are batting .230 against him, and his performance against the Yankees came on a day when he had an unimpressive pregame warmup session, the kind that made his pitching coach wonder whether the ace was going to survive the early innings.

"You know how you hear those bullpen stories?" said Sox pitching coach Dave Wallace, recalling tales of pitchers who rediscover strength during the walk from the bullpen to the mound. "Today was one of them."

The happy ending came at a good time, too, for Martinez and the Red Sox alike. Entering the game against the Yankees, the Sox were 4-9 in Martinez' previous 13 starts against

the Yankees, a record that included Games 3 and 7 of last year's American League Championship Series. Martinez was roundly booed when he stepped onto the field, the reception prompting him to flash a smile at catcher Jason Varitek.

After the 12-inning marathon on April 24 in which skipper Terry Francona emptied out his bullpen, the Sox needed Martinez to respond. They needed him to stay on the mound and to give them a chance to win, and Martinez did both. He made it through the first three innings in 34 pitches, a number that became all the more important when he labored through the fourth (25 pitches) and fifth (24).

In his final two innings, Martinez threw 22 pitches, including just eight in a seventh inning that brought him to his magic number of 105.

"I think he's just a good pitcher," Francona said of Martinez' ability to conserve pitches. "And when he pitches good, I think you're going to see results like that."

Four seasons ago, when the Red Sox last swept a three-game series at Yankee Stadium, Martinez began the weekend with a one-hit gem in which he struck out 17 and faced just 28 batters. It was one of the greatest games ever pitched. Martinez' effort will not rank anywhere near that masterpiece, but the Martinez of today is producing a different kind of work.

"Every win is important," Martinez said in a statement (in English) issued by the Sox after the game. "These are the people we're behind [historically], so it's nice to take advantage of these opportunities against them."

SOX PICK UP WHERE THEY LEFT OFF VS. A'S

BY JEFF HORRIGAN, BOSTON HERALD

The Oakland A's vowed revenge last Oct. 6, when they interpreted Derek Lowe's celebratory hand gesture after recording the final out in the decisive fifth game of the American League

	1	2	3		4	5	6		7	8	9		R	H	E
Oakland	0	0	0		0	0	1		1	0	0		2	10	0
Boston	1	0	1		3	4	0		3	0	X		12	19	0

Oakland	AB	R	H	RBI
Kotsay, CF	5	0	1	1
Byrnes, LF	4	1	1	0
Chavez, 3B	4	0	1	1
Dye, RF	4	0	0	0
Hatteberg, 1B	4	0	1	0
Durazo, DH	4	1	2	0
Crosby, SS	4	0	1	0
Melhuse, C	3	0	0	0
Kielty, PH	1	0	1	0
McLemore, 2B	3	0	2	0
Scutaro, 2B	1	0	0	0
Totals	37	2	10	2

Boston	AB	R	H	RBI
Damon, CF	6	2	3	0
Bellhorn, 2B	6	4	3	5
Ortiz, DH	6	2	4	2
Ramirez, LF	4	2	2	3
Dominique, 1B	1	0	0	0
Daubach, 1B	1	0	0	0
McCarty, PH-LF	1	0	1	0
Varitek, C	3	0	3	1
Millar, RF	4	0	0	0
Kapler, RF	0	0	0	1
Youkilis, 3B	2	2	1	0
Reese, SS	4	0	2	0
Crespo, PH-SS	1	0	0	0
Totals	39	12	19	12

2B: Durazo, Byrnes, Chavez, Ortiz 2, Ramirez, Varitek, Bellhorn, Youkilis; HR: Ramirez (12), Bellhorn (6).

Oakland	IP	H	R	ER	BB	SO
Hudson (L, 5-2)	4.0	9	5	5	4	2
Hammond	2.0	5	4	4	1	1
Rincon	0.2	4	3	3	2	1
Duchscherer	1.1	1	0	0	0	3

Boston	IP	H	R	ER	BB	SO
Schilling (W, 6-3)	7.0	9	2	2	0	5
Dinardo	1.0	0	0	0	0	1
Brown	1.0	1	0	0	0	2

WP: Hudson; HBP: Daubach (by Hudson), Youkilis (by Hudson); T: 3:15; Att: 35,236.

Division Series as a crude attempt to insult them.

After a seven-and-a-half month wait, however, their first attempt to attain retribution ended up being even more humiliating than the message they perceived from an excited pitcher's exultation.

The Sox, who stunned the A's last October by rallying from an 0-2 deficit in the best-of-five series, let their bats inflict the indignation leading to a 12-2 pounding at Fenway Park. The defeat ended the A's five-game winning streak.

The Sox treated Tim Hudson, one of the game's top hurlers, like a batting-practice pitcher and recorded season highs in runs and hits (19). Hudson, who fell to 1-3 with an 8.53 ERA during the regular season at Fenway, was hammered for five runs on nine hits, including five doubles, in only four innings.

He walked four batters, hit two others and uncorked a wild pitch (only the second of the year for Oakland).

David Ortiz matched a career high with four hits, while Mark Bellhorn went 3-for-6 with a home run, double, five RBIs and a career-high four runs scored. Johnny Damon and Jason

ABOVE: Sox David Ortiz and Manny Ramirez point skyward after Ramirez nails a two-run home run in the fifth inning. (Matthew West/Boston Herald)

Varitek had three hits apiece, and Manny Ramirez belted his team-leading 12th homer.

Sox pitcher Curt Schilling, who has been in search of consistency over the past month, turned in his second consecutive strong start. Schilling (6-3) allowed two runs on nine scattered hits over seven innings, while striking out five batters and walking none.

The Sox improved their major league-leading home record to 15-6 with their 11th win at Fenway in their last 14 games.

Hudson entered the game as Oakland's all-time leader in winning percentage (.714, 85-34), but he wasn't even been mediocre last night.

The Red Sox jumped on him in the first inning but squandered opportunities to blow it open early. Back-to-back two-out doubles by Ortiz and Ramirez made it 1-0, but Boston left the bases loaded.

Varitek made it 2-0 in the third with a two-out double lined to the right field corner, but the Sox left runners at second and third bases.

Hudson, who came into the game leading the league in fewest pitches per inning, threw a whopping 92 last night, including 41 in his fourth and final frame.

The Sox left the bases loaded again in the fourth inning, but they still managed to tack on three more runs, extending the lead to 5-0 and driving Hudson from the game.

Bellhorn knocked in a pair of runs with a double smashed to the left-center field gap, and Ortiz pushed him across with a two-bagger that caromed off the base of the center field wall on a hop.

The Sox blew it open in the fourth against former Yankees lefty Hammond by piling on four more runs. Ramirez' 12th homer of the season, a blast into the Green Monster seats, made it 9-0.

Schilling coasted through the first five innings before losing his shutout bid in the sixth on consecutive, one-out doubles by Eric Byrnes and Eric Chavez.

LEFT: Sox Kevin Youkilis is hit by a Tim Hudson pitch in the fourth inning. Hudson was expected to dominate the Sox batting order; instead the Sox scored five runs on nine hits in four innings. (Matthew West/Boston Herald)

ABOVE: Sox starter Curt Schilling found consistency against the A's, allowing two runs on nine hits over seven innings. He struck out five batters and walked none. (Matthew West/Boston Herald)

MANNY RAMIREZ

MANNY RAMIREZ • OUTFIELD • MANNY RAMIREZ • OUTFIELD • MANNY RAMIRE
TFIELD • M   Y R   Z • OU   D •   Y R   F L   • MA
IREZ •   T   ITFIELD
N RAMI   OUT   •   Y RA   •
TFIELD •   MANNY RAMIREZ • OUTFIELD • MANNY RAMIREZ • OUTFIELD • MAN

BY KAREN GUREGIAN

These days, being around Manny Ramirez is like watching the Discovery Channel. Almost every time you tune in, you learn something new about the Red Sox slugger.

It could be something small and somewhat humorous, like finding out he shops at Men's Warehouse, or some headline screamer-like offering to surrender part of his contract to keep Pedro Martinez in town.

Yesterday's pearl falls somewhere in between. A wonderfully introspective Ramirez indicated he was strongly leaning toward retiring when his contract with the club expires.

The Sox star is midway through the eight-year, $160 million monster pact he inked with the Dan Duquette regime in December 2000. And no, this has nothing to do with how he feels about playing in Boston.

Basically, it comes down to the usual issue that tugs at ballplayers' hearts: Family.

Ramirez, who turns 32 on May 30, is no different than most professional athletes with small children. He wants to spend more quality time with his two sons.

The Sox outfielder hates being away for extended periods of time from his wife, Juliana, and their 2-year-old son, Manuel. Ramirez' 8-year-old son, Manny, whom he fathered from a prior relationship, also lives with the couple in their Fort Lauderdale, Fla., home.

"I got my kids. I'm away from home so much. I want to see them grow up, you know what I mean?" Ramirez said. "That's why I'm thinking about that. It's hard. You've got your family, you're always away from them, and you don't get to see your kids."

During the recent road trip to Cleveland, proud papa Ramirez would sit at his locker and pull out pictures of his family to show old friends. At one point, he casually tossed out his future retirement plans.

Sure, it's possible he could change his mind between now and 2008 or beyond—the Sox hold options on 2009 and 2010—but right now, the six-time All-Star and arguably the best hitter in baseball is of the mindset he'll put a cap on his career when the contract expires.

"I might feel different [in time], but it's hard when you have your family, and you're all over the place, and you don't see your kids grow up," Ramirez said. "You always have it on your mind."

Once again, this is another side of Manny fans haven't been privy to since he made Boston his second home. That of loving father.

Ramirez also made it perfectly clear he wanted to be a Red Sox for the duration of his career. Being put on irrevocable waivers during the winter, and being involved in the unsuccessful Alex Rodriguez swap haven't altered his opinion of playing here.

"I definitely want to finish in Boston," Ramirez said. "This is the place to be. If you're going to win a World Series, this is the place to do it. Not New York, not Miami, that's nothing. The big thing is winning here, and we've got the pieces to do it this year, and I think we're going to do it."

ORTIZ OFFENSE DELIVERS AS SOX DODGE A BULLET

BY JEFF HORRIGAN, BOSTON HERALD

Manny Ramirez is typically a man of few words, so when the Red Sox left fielder dropped a wind-blown fly ball with two outs in the top of the ninth inning to squander a 1-0 lead, his teammates weren't expecting to hear much when he returned to the bench.

	1	2	3		4	5	6		7	8	9		R	H	E
Los Angeles	0	0	0		0	0	0		0	0	1		1	7	0
Boston	0	0	0		0	0	0		1	0	1		2	7	1

Los Angeles	AB	R	H	RBI
Roberts, LF	4	0	2	0
Saenz, PH	1	0	0	0
Werth, PR-LF	0	0	0	0
Izturis, SS	4	0	0	0
Bradley, CF	2	0	1	0
Green, DH	4	0	1	0
Lo Duca, C	4	0	1	0
Beltre, 3B	3	0	0	0
Encarnacion, RF	4	0	0	0
Ventura, 1B	3	0	1	0
Hernandez, PR-1B	0	0	0	0
Grabowski, PH-1B	1	0	0	0
Cora, 2B	3	1	1	0
Totals	33	1	7	0

Boston	AB	R	H	RBI
Damon, CF	3	1	1	0
Bellhorn, 2B	4	0	1	0
Ortiz, DH	4	1	3	2
Ramirez, LF	3	0	0	0
Varitek, C	3	0	0	0
Millar, RF	3	0	0	0
Kapler, RF	0	0	0	0
Youkilis, 3B	2	0	1	0
McCarty, 1B	3	0	0	0
Reese, SS	3	0	1	0
Totals	28	2	7	2

2B: Bellhorn; HR: Ortiz (13); SB: Bradley, Roberts, Reese; E: Ramirez.

Los Angeles	IP	H	R	ER	BB	SO
Perez, O	8.0	5	1	1	1	7
Martin (L, 0-1)	0.0	2	1	1	1	0

Boston	IP	H	R	ER	BB	SO
Lowe	7.0	5	0	0	4	4
Timlin	1.0	1	0	0	0	1
Foulke (W, 2-0)	1.0	1	1	0	0	1

T: 2:32; Att: 35,173.

When he reached David Ortiz, however, Ramirez stopped, shook his head and muttered: "There goes my Gold Glove."

The unexpected remark cracked up Ortiz, but minutes later, the Boston designated hitter allowed Ramirez to have the last laugh. Ramirez' misplay of Olmedo Saenz' two-out fly ball allowed the Los Angeles Dodgers to tie the score, but Ortiz sent the Sox to a 2-1 victory at Fenway Park with a run-scoring single off Tom Martin in the bottom half of the inning.

"Manny picks us up many times," Ortiz said. "Now it's our time to pick him up."

The win was the Sox' fifth in the last six games as they improved to 3-1 in interleague play.

Red Sox starter Derek Lowe tossed seven shutout innings (five hits, four strikeouts) in his best outing of the season and Mike Timlin followed with a scoreless eighth to set up Keith Foulke to save what would have been the Sox' second 1-0 win in four games.

Foulke retired the first two batters in the ninth before Alex Cora reached safely on an infield single knocked down by diving second baseman Mark Bellhorn. Pinch-hitter Saenz fol-

ABOVE: Sox starter Derek Lowe pitched seven shutout innings allowing only five hits against the Dodgers. He struck out four batters in what has been his best outing of the season thus far. (Kevin Wisniewski/Boston Herald)

lowed with a towering fly to shallow left field that got caught up in a gust and confounded a looping Ramirez. He stuck his glove out at the last second to make a basket catch, but the ball fell to the turf.

"I went back, the ball kept coming in and I just dropped the ball," Ramirez said.

"I gave it my best and I just dropped the ball. I felt bad. That's why you've got teammates, to go out and pick you up."

Cora raced around to score the tying run as the 95th consecutive Fenway sellout fell into a stunned hush. Foulke, who was saddled with his second blown save, looked skyward for an answer that wasn't there.

"I almost started bawling," Sox manager Terry Francona said. "That's about as close to tears as I've been in a long time."

The Sox had little luck against Los Angeles starter Odalis Perez, other than Ortiz' 13th homer of the season, which he lined into the visitors bullpen leading off the seventh to break a scoreless tie.

Perez, who has had 11 of his 13 starts this season decided by one or two runs, surrendered only five hits in eight innings, while striking out seven. When Dodgers manager Jim Tracy called on lefty Martin to start the bottom of the ninth, Ramirez wasn't the only one letting out a huge sigh of relief.

"Manny's going to win us more games than he's going to lose," Lowe said, vindicating Ramirez for his squandered win.

Ramirez, however, never got a chance to vindicate himself. Martin walked leadoff man Johnny Damon and Bellhorn followed with a double lined to the left field corner that put runners on second and third with no outs. With the dangerous Ramirez on deck, Tracy took a chance with the southpaw facing the left-handed Ortiz.

Martin jumped ahead of Ortiz, 0-and-2, before the slugger turned on a breaking ball and drove it down the right field line to knock in Damon with the game-winning run.

Ramirez was left on the on-deck circle with a bat in his hands.

"It wouldn't have surprised me if David Ortiz hadn't gotten a hit, Manny would have hit one off the wall, or over," Francona said.

LEFT: Sox outfielder Manny Ramirez drops a fly ball with two outs in the ninth inning. The error allowed the Dodgers to tie the game. (Kevin Wisniewski/Boston Herald)

ABOVE: Sox players congratulate David Ortiz on his game-winning hit against the Dodgers that put the Sox up 2-1. (Kevin Wisniewski/Boston Herald)

"Manny picks us up many times. Now it's our time to pick him up."

—David Ortiz

SOX COME OFF ROPES TO DELIVER KNOCKOUT

BY MICHAEL SILVERMAN, BOSTON HERALD

The Red Sox and the Yankees served a bloody reminder that tensions in their eons-long war are as high as ever by engaging in yet another benches-clearing brawl, this one involving Alex Rodriguez and Jason Varitek in the third inning.

Tempers are one thing. Winning is another, and unlike last year's melee-intensive Game 3 of the American League Championship Series, the home team came out on top.

It took a game-winning two-run home run in the bottom of the ninth by Bill Mueller off the best closer in the game, Mariano Rivera, to lift the Red Sox to an 11-10 victory, one that the team prays will be paying dividends far beyond a single day.

"It's a huge win for us, and it will be bigger if we make it bigger," said manager Terry Francona, who was one of five to get ejected from the game. "If we have this catapult us and we do something with it, that's what will really make it big."

This game almost got pushed back to September after heavy rains left the outfield a marsh. The Red Sox, Yankees and umpiring crew came close to calling the game, but a lobbying effort from Red Sox players helped convince the team to get the game in. They did, 54 minutes late.

	1	2	3	4	5	6	7	8	9	R	H	E
NY Yankees	0	2	1	0	0	6	1	0	0	10	12	0
Boston	0	0	2	2	0	4	0	0	3	11	15	4

NY Yankees	AB	R	H	RBI
Williams, CF	6	2	2	0
Jeter, SS	4	1	1	0
Sheffield, RF	4	0	0	1
Rodriguez, 3B	1	1	0	0
Wilson, PR-2B	3	1	2	2
Posada, C	4	2	2	0
Matsui, LF	5	1	3	3
Sierra, R., DH	5	1	1	1
Clark, 1B	5	0	0	1
Cairo, 2B-3B	5	1	1	1
Totals	**42**	**10**	**12**	**9**

Boston	AB	R	H	RBI
Damon, CF	5	0	2	2
Varitek, C	1	0	0	0
Mirabelli, C	4	0	0	0
Ortiz, DH	3	1	1	0
Ramirez, LF	4	1	1	1
Garciaparra, SS	5	2	3	2
Nixon, RF	3	1	1	0
Millar, 1B	5	2	4	1
McCarty, PR	0	1	0	0
Mueller, 3B	4	2	2	3
Bellhorn, 2B	4	1	1	2
Totals	**38**	**11**	**15**	**11**

2B: Matsui 2, Williams, Posada, Mueller, Ramirez, Bellhorn, Garciaparra. HR: Sierra, R (13), Mueller (8); E: Arroyo, Mueller, Malaska, Garciaparra.

NY Yankees	IP	H	R	ER	BB	SO
Sturtze	3.0	2	2	2	0	2
Padilla	2.0	6	4	4	2	1
Quantrill	0.2	3	2	2	0	1
Heredia	0.0	0	0	0	2	0
Proctor	2.0	1	0	0	1	2
Rivera (L, 1-1)	0.2	3	3	3	0	0

Boston	IP	H	R	ER	BB	SO
Arroyo	5.2	10	8	6	0	4
Leskanic	0.0	1	1	1	3	0
Malaska	0.1	1	1	1	0	1
Embree	1.0	0	0	0	0	1
Mendoza (W, 1-0)	2.0	0	0	0	0	1

Balk: Proctor; HBP: Rodriguez (by Arroyo); T: 3:54 (:54 delay); Att: 34,501.

ABOVE: Sox Jason Varitek shoves Yankee Alex Rodriguez in the face, which started a bench-clearing brawl during the third inning. (AP/WWP)

ABOVE: As Yankee Derek Jeter cheers, Sox Johnny Damon protests the call at second after he is ruled out. (Tara Bricking/Boston Herald)

The Red Sox quickly fell into a 3-0 hole before the extended scrum session. It began when Rodriguez took offense at being plunked by Red Sox starter Bronson Arroyo. Varitek and Rodriguez began jawing at each other as the Yanks third baseman strolled slowly to first. Finally the Sox catcher had heard enough and began shoving A-Rod. All hell broke loose after that—New York starter Tanyon Sturtze was left with blood on his face after a tussle with Gabe Kapler—but there was still a hell of a baseball game left to play. The quality of play was far from pristine, especially with the Sox committing four errors, but the home team's initial

desire to play was rewarded in the most stirring fashion possible—a walkoff home run.

"You always build on positives and this is a positive. We came back, and like I keep saying over and over, you play for nine innings," Mueller said. "This game isn't five innings, it's not six innings. If there's a pause in the game, you put it behind you and you keep going."

For an underachieving team that has been struggling to play with intensity on a consistent basis all season long, Mueller's blast may wind up lending substance to a season's worth of talk about talent and effort.

"I'm very, very proud of what our players did today," Sox general manager Theo Epstein said. "This game had as much intensity, if not more, than a postseason game. If we go on to play like this, this will go down as one of the most important victories we had. Today was not about stats or box scores, it was about emotions."

The Red Sox battled back from an early 3-0 hole and then lost a 4-3 lead when the Yankees scored six times in the sixth to go up, 9-4. The Sox drew to within one at 9-8 in the bottom of the sixth before the Yanks added a run in the seventh.

The Sox had thrown some punches in the third, but they delivered the knockout in the ninth.

"You're never out of it if you continue to fight," Francona said. "I hope this day, we look back awhile from now and we're saying that this brought us together."

> **"It's a huge win for us, and it will be bigger if we make it bigger. If we have this catapult us and we do something with it, that's what will really make it big."**
>
> **—Terry Francona**

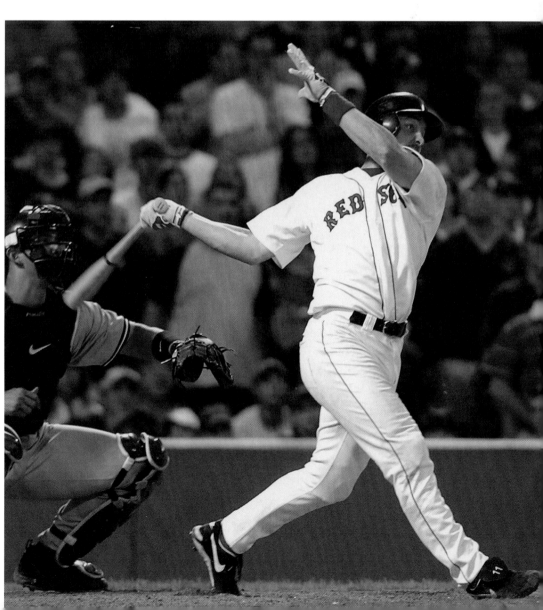

RIGHT: Sox Bill Mueller hits a walk-off two-run homer to win the game against the Yankees in the ninth inning. (Tara Bricking/Boston Herald)

TIM WAKEFIELD • PITCHER • TIM WAKEFIELD • PITCHER • TIM WAKEFIELD • PITCHER • TIM WAKEFIELD • PITCH
TIM WAKEFIELD • PITCHER • TIM WAKEFIELD • PITCHER • TIM WAKEFIELD • PITCHER • TIM WAKEFIELD • PITCH
TIM WAKEFIELD • PITCHER • TIM WAKEFIELD • PITCHER • TIM WAKEFIELD • PITCHER • TIM WAKEFIELD • PITCHER • PITC
TIM WAKEFIELD • PITCHER • TIM WAKEFIELD • PITCHER • TIM WAKEFIELD • PITCHER • TIM WAKEFIELD • PITCI

TIM WAKEFIELD

BY MIKE SHALIN

On a night of personal milestones, Tim Wakefield was thrilled the Red Sox got a win.

"As a whole, team-wise, it's a huge win for us, coming off the two losses in Minnesota and coming into Tampa, [which] is actually no slouch," the knuckleballer said after his seven solid innings paced the Sox' 6-3 win over the Devil Rays. "It's always important to win the first game of a series."

For Wakefield, this particular win—his 10th in 11 career decisions against the Devil Rays (he also has three saves against them)—was big because it came on his 38th birthday. It also came in his 239th Red Sox start, moving him past Luis Tiant for third place on the club's all-time list.

Wakefield also pitched the 2,000th inning of his major league career last night—not bad for a guy who started out as an infielder.

"Oh, I did? Oh, wow," he said. "That's nice. I didn't know that."

He also didn't know why he's had so much success against Tampa.

"Lucky, I guess," he said.

But there were at least two things he did know. He knew he threw a bad pitch that Tino Martinez, 11-for-33 with a homer and six RBIs against Wakefield coming in, hit into the right field seats for a 2-0 Devil Rays lead in the first inning. He also knew he had to hold the other guys down after David McCarty answered Martinez' shot with a three-run job in the top of the second.

"It's motivating for me, knowing that it's very important to get my offense back in the dugout again," Wakefield said of being given the lead right back. "You hone your concentration in a little bit harder knowing that they just came back and took the lead back from them. The concentration's gotta be a little bit better."

Once the Sox took the lead, Wakefield got very stingy. The knuckler got the next two batters after the homer to end the first inning. He then retired the next eight, until Jose Cruz singled with two out in the fourth. Julio Lugo walked, but Toby Hall grounded out to end the threat.

A nifty stop by Kevin Youkilis at third helped Wakefield out in the fifth, and the knuckleballer allowed one single over his final two innings.

The result was his second straight win since his July 17 start in Anaheim, Calif., when he got nailed on the right shoulder blade by a line drive. Red Sox manager Terry Francona said "he still feels it," but Wakefield insists all is well.

"I'm past that," he said. "Our training staff's done a great job keeping me limber and able to throw. . . . The last start in Baltimore I was achy a little bit, but I'm feeling a lot better now and I don't feel any ill effects from that."

Nancy lane/boston herald

TRADING DEADLINE

TRADING DEADLINE • TRADING DEADLINE • TRADING DEADLINE • TRADING DEADLINE
ADING DEADLINE • TRADING DEADLINE • TRADING DEADLINE • TRADING DEADLIN
ADING DEADLINE • TRADING DEADLINE • TRADING DEADLINE • TRADING DEADLIN
ADING DEADLINE • TRADING DEADLINE • TRADING DEADLINE • TRADING DEADLIN
ADING DEADLINE • TRADING DEADLINE • TRADING DEADLINE • TRADING DEADLIN

BY MICHAEL SILVERMAN

Hoping to build a defense strong enough to win the World Series, the Red Sox traded away an icon: Nomar Garciaparra.

To call the trade a whopper or a blockbuster or jaw-dropping is no understatement. Four teams were involved. Garciaparra went to the Chicago Cubs, while the Red Sox received two Gold Glovers, first baseman Doug Mientkiewicz from the Minnesota Twins and shortstop Orlando Cabrera from the Montreal Expos. Along with Garciaparra, the Red Sox sent Single-A outfielder Matt Murton and cash considerations to the Cubs.

In a separate deal, the Sox acquired speedy outfielder Dave Roberts from the Los Angeles Dodgers for Triple-A outfielder Henri Stanley.

Moving Garciaparra, a five-time All-Star, two-time batting champion and 1997 Rookie of the Year, was always a possibility as the trading deadline approached, yet most felt the Red Sox would be unable to improve the team significantly enough to endure the loss of their shortstop.

But Garciaparra's impending free agency and his lingering resentment over the team's attempt to deal him last offseason for Alex Rodriquez contributed to the thinking on Yawkey Way. The most important factor, however, was general manager Theo Epstein's desire to improve the team's sub-par defense.

"You never want to trade a player of Nomar Garciaparra's caliber," Epstein said at a Fenway Park press conference. "But in moving a player like Nomar—we're deep in the season—

four months in and as much as I like the club, I'm responsible for the flaws on the team that we could not allow to become a fatal flaw. Our defense has not been championship-caliber. In my mind, we're not going to win a championship with this defense. We're a well-rounded club now."

Garciaparra, penciled into the starting line-up, had nearly finished putting on his Red Sox uniform when he was notified of the trade after the 3 p.m. local deadline. Shortly thereafter, the clubhouse was closed. When it re-opened, Garciaparra was in his street clothes, saying his goodbyes and getting ready to catch a plane to Chicago.

"There's definitely a little sadness—I'm leaving a place I love," Garciaparra said. "What we had on the field was pretty special. Off the field, I'll never forget the way the fans embraced me."

Starter Pedro Martinez was downcast after exchanging cell-phone numbers with Garciaparra.

"It's always sad to see a superstar leave," Martinez said. "He, [Tim] Wakie and I were the last old goats. I'm sad. I imagine he's a little sad.

Left fielder Manny Ramirez had a matter-of-fact view of the transaction. "That's baseball—that's why you don't fall in love with any team," he said. "He's the best hitter I've ever seen. He's going to be awesome out there."

Asked if the team will be better, Martinez said, "I have no idea, I have to see it in play. I know what Nomar can do."

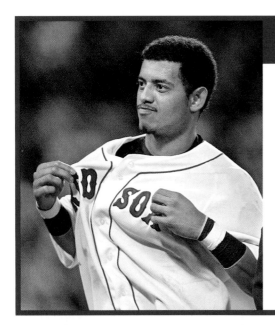

ORLANDO CABRERA

Shortstop   44

Bats right and throws right...Born November 2, 1974 in Cartagena, Columbia...Made his major-league debut on September 3, 1997...In his six seasons with the Expos (1997-2003), was twice chosen as the team's most valuable player...Won a Gold Glove at SS in 2001

(Matt Stone/Boston Herald)

DOUG MIENTKIEWICZ

First Baseman   13

Bats left and throws right...Born June 19, 1974 in Toledo, Ohio...Made his major-league debut on September 18, 1998...Member of the United States Olympic gold-medal-winning team in 2000 in Sydney...Played for the Minnesota Twins from 1998 through 2004...Hit better than .300 twice (2001 and 2003)...Won a Gold Glove at 1B in 2001

(Michael Seamans/Boston Herald)

DAVE ROBERTS

Outfielder   31

Bats left and throws left...Born May 31, 1972 in Okinawa, Japan...Made his major-league debut on August 7, 1999...Played for three season with Cleveland before joining the Dodgers...Registered more than 40 steals in two consecutive seasons (2002 and 2003)...Played flawless defense in 2002, successfully handling all 256 chances for a 1.000 fielding percentage

(Stuart Cahill/Boston Herald)

RED SOX POWER
SURGE GIVES JAYS
A JOLT

BY JEFF HORRIGAN, BOSTON HERALD

With the exception of Kevin Millar, who had agreed to give one of Norm Abram's homemade bats a test run, few of the Red Sox seemed to take notice when the master carpenter from *This*

Toronto	1 2 3	4 5 6	7 8 9	R	H	E
Toronto	0 0 0	1 0 0	3 0 0	4	6	1
Boston	0 1 0	2 2 0	0 3 X	8	10	2

Toronto	AB	R	H	RBI
Rios, RF	4	0	0	0
Hudson, 2B	4	1	3	0
Wells, CF	4	0	1	1
Delgado, 1B	1	1	0	0
Catalanotto, DH	4	0	0	0
Hinske, 3B	4	1	1	0
Woodward, SS	4	1	0	0
Gross, LF	4	0	1	1
Cash, C	2	0	0	0
Zaun, PH-C	1	0	0	0
Totals	32	4	6	2

Boston	AB	R	H	RBI
Damon, CF	5	1	2	2
Roberts, RF-LF	4	1	1	1
Ramirez, LF	5	2	2	0
Kapler, RF	0	0	0	0
Ortiz, DH	3	2	1	0
Millar, 1B	2	0	1	2
Gutierrez, PR-2B	1	0	0	0
Varitek, C	2	0	0	1
Cabrera, SS	3	0	1	2
Mueller, 3B	2	1	1	0
Mientkiewicz, 2B-1B	4	1	1	0
Totals	31	8	10	8

2B: Hudson, Ortiz, Ramirez, Millar, Mientkiewicz, Roberts; 3B: Damon; SB: Hudson, Woodward, Mueller; E: Hudson, Cabrera.

Toranto	IP	H	R	ER	BB	SO
Miller (L, 1-2)	4.1	6	5	4	5	1
Douglass	1.2	0	0	0	2	2
Speier	1.0	0	0	0	1	3
Chulk	0.0	3	3	3	0	0
Ligtenberg	1.0	1	0	0	1	0

Boston	IP	H	R	ER	BB	SO
Lowe (W, 11-10)	7.0	5	4	3	1	7
Foulke (S, 20)	2.0	1	0	0	1	2

WP: Speier; HBP: Delgado (by Lowe); T: 2:59; Att: 35,271.

Old House made an appearance on the field prior to the game at Fenway Park.

While the Sox are typically more concerned with OPS than PBS, Abram had to have appreciated the way the club went out and converted a somewhat ugly effort into a nice 8-4 win over the Toronto Blue Jays at the game's oldest ballpark.

The Sox made good use of the lumber, pounding five Toronto pitchers for 10 hits, while Derek Lowe, the one most likely to benefit from a change of scenery, avoided a hammering and tossed seven strong innings to win for the second straight start and the fourth time in five decisions.

Lowe (11-10) allowed three earned runs on five hits and a hit batsman, while equaling a season high with seven strikeouts. The impending free agent, who was last over .500 on June 17 (6-5), nearly blew his effort after a retaliatory plunking of Carlos Delgado in the seventh

OPPOSITE: Sox third baseman Bill Mueller makes contact in the second inning. The Sox were able to stay ahead of the Blue Jays 8-4. (Douglas McFadd/Boston Herald)

inning led to a three-run Toronto rally, narrowing his once-comfortable lead to 5-4.

The Sox, however, responded with three runs in the eighth inning to provide breathing room for Keith Foulke, who pitched the final two innings to record his 20th save.

"This whole second half, I feel like I've given this team a chance to win pretty much every time, whereas the first half, it was kind of not even hit or miss," Lowe said. "It was more miss."

Doug Mientkiewicz, who played well in his first career start at second base, was impressed by Lowe's sinker, which led to 19-of-21 outs via grounders or strikeouts.

"When he's got his stuff, he's one of the nastiest guys in the American League," Mientkiewicz said. "That's the Derek Lowe I didn't want to see when I was facing him."

Eight of nine starters collected hits for Boston, which won for the seventh time in 10 games and improved to 5-3 on the 10-game homestand.

Playing second for the second time in his career, Mientkiewicz made a great play to turn a

The Sox broke open a 1-1 tie with two runs in both the fourth and fifth innings and never trailed again. Jason Varitek put the Sox ahead for the duration with a fourth-inning sacrifice fly while Millar belted a bases-loaded, two-run double off the Green Monster to knock Toronto starter Justin Miller (1-2) out of the game.

With a four-run lead, Lowe extracted some revenge for Mientkiewicz by plunking Delgado in the right hip with a first-pitch fastball in the seventh. It led to a three-run rally that briefly cut the Sox' lead to a run, but Lowe's new teammate appreciated the gesture.

"That brings clubs together when you stick up for one of your own," Mientkiewicz said. "I tried to tell him it's part of the game, but Derek took it upon himself."

double play on Vernon Wells' grounder in the first. Things didn't go as smoothly in the second inning, however. Mientkiewicz fielded the ball and went to tag runner Carlos Delgado as he ran toward second, only to be flattened by a vicious forearm, preventing him from completing another double play.

"On one hand, he played the game the way it's supposed to be played," Mientkiewicz said. "He played it hard, and there's nothing dirty about it. I just felt he knew I'm not a second baseman, and I don't appreciate the fact that he took advantage of it. I don't think it's a cheap shot, but let's put it this way, I wouldn't do that to [a guy] who was playing his first game at second base."

" **When he's got his stuff, he's one of the nastiest guys in the American League. That's the Derek Lowe I didn't want to see when I was facing him.** "

—Doug Mientkiewicz

BELOW: Sox Doug Mientkiewicz (13) collides with Toronto Blue Jays runner Carlos Delgado to make a play at second base. It was only Mientkiewicz' second time playing second base in his career. (Douglas McFadd/Boston Herald)

JASON VARITEK

BY MICHAEL SILVERMAN

Jason Varitek is hitting the ball so hard and playing the game so well, it is next to impossible to imagine the Red Sox being without him for four days in 2004 as it is to being without him in 2005 and beyond.

Varitek's two home runs for the Red Sox in a 10-7 victory over the White Sox were each stark reminders of how hot his bat has become this month. In the August, the catcher leads the team in batting average (.444) and RBIs (18)—plus he has five home runs.

If there is one person to point your finger at in the Red Sox clubhouse for spearheading the 13-6 August surge, it's Varitek.

Yet sometime soon, word is likely to get out that Varitek will not opt to appeal his four-game suspension for throwing the first glove in the Alex Rodriguez' how-dare-you-hit-me-Bronson-Arroyo episode at Fenway on July 24. Instead, it looks as if a four-day, four-game game stretch squeezed in between Pedro Martinez starts this week, with the club playing relative lightweights in the Toronto Blue Jays and Detroit Tigers, will serve as Varitek's down time. Martinez is scheduled to go on Aug. 23 in Toronto and on Aug. 28 at home against Detroit.

"We'll try to do it when it would best help the team to do it, period," said Varitek.

While Gabe Kapler has no intention of dropping his appeal of a two-game ban pertaining to the same incident, Varitek's appeal is still scheduled to be heard Aug. 26, with the suspension to begin immediately afterward. Since the club would need to make a transaction in order to bring up a backup catcher, someone would have to come down with an injury. But just as important, serving the suspension would mean Varitek would miss at least one game of the Anaheim Angels series at Fenway Park that begins Aug. 31. There is no way the wild card-chasing club wants to be without Varitek for one game in that all-important series, which is followed by three games with the Texas Rangers, also a wild card wannabe.

"Maybe 'Tek will get the flu," said manager Terry Francona with a wry smile, referencing Rodriguez' bout with the flu earlier this month when the Yankees third baseman decided to drop his appeal.

So while everyone will be on the lookout for signs of a runny nose from Varitek in Toronto after Martinez' start, he has two more games to bulk up his already ample August accomplishments.

On a day when the wind was blowing in from center field, Varitek's first home run came in the fifth inning off of right-hander Jon Adkins. It was a line drive that simply tore through the heavy chop, sailing over the center field wall. The switch-hitting catcher went opposite-field, to left, on his solo shot leading off the seventh. In his last at-bat in the ninth, he gave a good go at home run No. 3 but the ball was caught on the warning track in right.

"Everything he does is meaningful to the club but his swing is so short and crisp, and his swing is so strong to begin with, when he swings like he has and we can put him in the middle of the lineup, it's such a plus for us," Francona said.

David Goldman/Boston Herald

HALO, NO!
SOX WON'T GO

BY JEFF HORRIGAN, BOSTON HERALD

Only time will tell if the Red Sox will complete their amazing comeback and catch the New York Yankees in the American League East race, but they are in the process of doing the next best thing to assure themselves a berth in the postseason.

Derek Lowe rebounded from a shaky beginning to pitch 7 1/3 solid innings, leading the Sox

to a three-game series sweep of the Anaheim Angels with a 4-3 victory at Fenway Park. Their ninth straight win knocked the Angels, who are their closest competitors in the wild card standings, 4 1/2 games off the pace.

"Sweeping a team like the Angels, we definitely didn't expect that," said Johnny Damon, who went 9-for-14 (.643) in the series. "They're the best team we've faced all season."

The Sox can pretty much polish off the wild card hopes of the Texas Rangers, who arrive in town for a three-game series trailing by six games after losing to Minnesota.

"No disrespect to the teams that we've played, but everyone kept saying, 'They've won a lot of games but look who they've played,'" said Lowe (13-10), who won his fourth consecutive decision by allowing three runs on seven hits. "Now we're playing the Anaheim Angels, who had won the same amount of games that we had, and then we win three in a row. I hope people start giving us credit, because this is a very special run that we are going on."

After scoring 22 runs the previous two nights, the Sox needed each and every one of their four runs. The teams traded tallies in each half of the first three frames before Bill Mueller

	1	2	3	4	5	6	7	8	9	R	H	E
Anaheim	1	1	1	0	0	0	0	0	0	3	8	0
Boston	1	2	1	0	0	0	0	0	X	4	12	1

Anaheim	AB	R	H	RBI
Eckstein, SS	4	0	0	0
Erstad, 1B	4	1	2	0
Guerrero, RF	4	1	1	0
Anderson, CF	4	0	1	2
Guillen, LF	4	0	0	0
Glaus, DH	4	0	1	0
Kennedy, 2B	4	1	2	0
Molina, J., C	2	0	1	1
DaVanon, PH	1	0	0	0
Figgins, 3B	3	0	0	0
Totals	34	3	8	3

Boston	AB	R	H	RBI
Damon, CF	4	1	3	1
Bellhorn, 2B	4	0	2	0
Ramirez, LF	5	0	0	0
Varitek, C	4	0	1	0
Millar, DH	4	0	1	1
Cabrera, SS	4	1	1	0
Mientkiewicz, 1B	3	1	1	0
Mueller, 3B	3	1	1	2
Roberts, RF	4	1	2	0
Kapler, RF	0	0	0	0
Totals	35	4	12	4

2B: Anderson, J. Molina, Erstad, Damon, Millar, Roberts 2, Mientkiewicz, Bellhorn 2; 3B: Kennedy, HR: Mueller (10); SB: Guerrero, Kennedy; E: Roberts.

Anaheim	IP	H	R	ER	BB	SO
Colon (L, 13-11)	4.2	10	4	4	4	5
Donnelly	1.1	1	0	0	2	2
Rodriguez	2.0	1	0	0	0	3

Boston	IP	H	R	ER	BB	SO
Lowe (W, 13-10)	7.1	7	3	3	1	6
Myers	0.1	0	0	0	0	0
Foulke (S, 26)	1.1	1	0	0	0	1

T: 3:17; Att: 35,050.

put the Sox ahead for the duration of the evening with a tiebreaking sacrifice fly in the bottom of the third. Mueller also belted his first home run since Aug. 4 in the second inning off Bartolo Colon (13-11).

"You look at our team and we play with intensity and we don't have many weaknesses right now," said right fielder Dave Roberts, who went 2-for-4 with a pair of doubles. "We have so many ways to beat you."

The win was the Sox' 15th in the last 16 games and their 18th in the last 21. They've won 10 straight at Fenway, marking their longest home winning streak since a 10-game run July 16-25, 1993. The overall winning streak is only the 33rd in club history of at least nine games and the longest since a nine-game streak April 30-May 9, 2002.

"For $150 million, this is how we're supposed to play," said closer Keith Foulke, who finished up with 1 1/3 scoreless innings for his 26th save of the season and his 12th successful save conversion in a row.

Boston, which has won its last five series, remained 3 1/2 games behind victorious New York in the AL East. The deficit hasn't been less than that since June 11, when they were 2 1/2 games back.

After bashing the ball in the previous two games of the series and capitalizing on nearly every scoring opportunity, the Sox left 14 runners on base last night and went just 2-for-14 at the plate with runners in scoring position.

ABOVE: Sox Bill Mueller makes a play to first as pitcher Derek Lowe ducks out of the way in the first inning. (Michael Seamans/Boston Herald)

ABOVE: Putting himself in scoring position in the first inning, Angel Vladimir Guerrero safely steals second under the tag of Sox shortstop Orlando Cabrera. (Michael Seamans/Boston Herald)

Orlando Cabrera and Mueller each struck out with the bases loaded to maroon three runners, but the Sox still managed to improve to 12-17 in one-run games, moving past Detroit (11) for the fewest such wins this season.

"We've said it over and over [that] you try to be one run better, regardless of how you do it," manager Terry Francona said. "There are times like tonight, when our pitching and our defense came through because we didn't spread it out when we had chances.

"We're all going to go home happy because our ball club together did good enough to beat them."

"No disrespect to the teams that we've played, but everyone kept saying, 'They've won a lot of games but look who they've played.' Now we're playing the Anaheim Angels, who had won the same amount of games that we had, and then we win three in a row. I hope people start giving us credit, because this is a very special run that we are going on."

—Derek Lowe

BELOW: Doug Mientkiewicz and Bill Mueller give Jason Varitek a high five after the Sox sweep the Angels, taking the last game of the series, 4-3. (Michael Seamans/Boston Herald)

KEITH FOULKE

KEITH FOULKE • PITCHER • KEITH FOULKE • PITCHER • KEITH FOULKE • PITCHER • PITCHE
ITH FOULKE • PIT KEITH FO E • P CHER • EITH FO A • PITCHER • KE
ULKE • PITCHER • KEITH FOULKE • PITCHER • EITH FOU E PITCHER • KEI
ULKE • PITCHER • KEITH FOULKE • PITCHER • KEITH FOU • PITCHER • KEI
ULKE • PITCHER • KEITH FOULKE • PITCHER • KEITH FOULKE • PITCHER • KE

BY MICHAEL SILVERMAN

More than any other reliever, a closer needs some kind of an outlet to turn to when the inevitable blown save comes his way.

The closer needs a way to blow off steam, to vent, to get rid of the stress and disappointment—not just to keep his sanity but also to be able to return to work the next day and be able to do his job again if asked.

Red Sox closer Keith Foulke came back to work from just such a day at the office Sept. 21 at Fenway Park, when he blew a save in the ninth inning by allowing a two-run home run to the Baltimore Orioles' Javy Lopez. Foulke would not get specific about how he did it, and in fact was a little touchy about having to talk at all about what happened after the save, but from the relaxed smile he had upon entering the clubhouse, he had forgotten as much as he needed to in order to handle the tasks at hand.

"I've got my own gig, there are things I do—I take care of it my own way," said Foulke, not saying when, how or where he lets off the steam.

However, the memory does not disappear. It just lingers less and less menacingly.

"It still bothers me," he said before the game against the Orioles. "It gets to me a lot, it tears me up, because the team worked so hard and they gave me the lead and I couldn't keep it."

Part of what made this particular blown save more bearable than others was that the Red Sox came back in the bottom of the ninth to walk off with a 3-2 victory. In one of those scoring rules that defy basic logic, Foulke even received the win.

But he got no joy out of it.

"When I go home and close my eyes at night, I remember the pitch and everything that happened," Foulke said. "It's not something that you forget. But still, I have to be ready today and do it again if I get called upon. That's my job. But I don't like talking about that stuff, even when I do get the save. Go talk to the guys who got me the lead. I'm boring."

The blown save was the sixth of the season for Foulke, a career-high, and his first since converting his 16 previous opportunities. He has 30 saves in all this season and sounded unamused that, in his opinion, he gets attention when he does something bad rather than good.

"When I blow a save, reporters always want to come up and ask some stupid question like, `What pitch was it?' when they know exactly what happened, what pitch it was—if they were watching the game," Foulke said. "They always want to talk to me when I screw up. When I do save a game, no one talks to me. But that's all right, too."

Everything's all right with Foulke now. He may or may not blow another save this season but if he does, he'll be fine. He'll make sure of it.

SOX GO WILD, CLINCH DATE WITH PLAYOFFS

BY JEFF HORRIGAN, BOSTON HERALD

After discovering that the magic number formula had played tricks on them, the Red Sox went out and defeated the Tampa Bay Devil Rays, 7-3, at Tropicana Field to establish a new magical number: 86.

That's the year—1986—that Boston last played in the World Series, as well as the number of years that have transpired since the Sox won their last championship in 1918.

Home runs by Johnny Damon, Manny Ramirez, Jason Varitek and David McCarty sent the Sox into the postseason for the second consecutive year and set off a spirited postgame celebration, albeit far more subdued than last year at Fenway Park.

"We haven't accomplished nothing yet," Ramirez said. "We're going to take it to another level now. . . . I think this is the year."

The Sox clinched at least the American League wild card slot, but they also moved within three games of the idle New York Yankees in the AL East with six games remaining. Any combination of New York wins or Boston losses totaling four will send the Sox to their seventh consecutive second-place finish.

	1 2 3	4 5 6	7 8 9	R	H	E
Boston	0 0 0	0 5 0	0 2 0	7	12	1
Tampa Bay	0 1 1	0 0 0	0 1 0	3	7	0

Boston	AB	R	H	RBI
Damon, CF	5	1	2	3
Bellhorn, 2B	5	1	1	0
Reese, 2B	0	0	0	0
Ramirez, DH	3	1	1	2
Hyzdu, PH-DH	0	0	0	0
Millar, LF	3	0	0	0
Roberts, LF	1	0	0	0
Varitek, C	5	1	2	1
Cabrera, SS	5	0	3	0
McCarty, 1B	4	2	2	1
Mientkiewicz, PH-1B	1	0	0	0
Youkilis, 3B	2	1	0	0
Kapler, RF	3	0	1	0
Totals	37	7	12	7

Tampa Bay	AB	R	H	RBI
Crawford, LF	4	1	2	0
Cruz, RF	3	0	0	0
Huff, 3B	1	0	0	0
Cantu, PR-2B	2	0	0	0
Baldelli, CF	3	0	0	1
Martinez, 1B	3	0	0	0
Cummings, DH	4	2	2	1
Lugo, SS	4	0	2	1
Blum, 2B-3B	4	0	0	0
Hall, C	4	0	1	0
Totals	32	3	7	3

2B: Bellhorn, Varitek, Lugo, Hall; HR: Damon (19), Ramirez (43), Varitek (18), McCarty (4), Cummings (2); E: Cabrera.

Boston	IP	H	R	ER	BB	SO
Arroyo (W, 10-9)	6.1	6	2	2	1	4
Myers	0.0	0	0	0	1	0
Leskanic	0.2	0	0	0	0	0
Timlin	1.0	1	1	1	0	0
Foulke	1.0	0	0	0	0	1

Tampa Bay	IP	H	R	ER	BB	SO
Kazmir	3.1	0	0	0	1	6
Sosa (L, 4-7)	1.0	4	5	5	1	1
Gaudin	2.2	2	0	0	1	3
Carter	0.2	4	2	2	0	1
Miller	0.1	1	0	0	0	1
Bell	1.0	0	0	0	1	0

WP: Arroyo; HBP: Huff (by Arroyo), Martinez (by Arroyo), Ramirez (by Kazmir), Millar (by Kazmir); T: 3:01 (:09 delay); Att: 17,602.

" You never forget your first time, but this is a different team than last year. We've had our own share of adversity. We were comatose for about three months, but the effort of these players pulling themselves out of it makes this really meaningful. **"**

—Theo Epstein

RIGHT: Sox pitcher Bronson Arroyo hurled a strong game, lasting for 6 1/3 innings and only giving up two runs. His win also gave the Sox pitching rotation five hurlers with more than 10 victories in a season since 1979. (AP/WWP)

ABOVE: Sox Johnny Damon (right) gets high fives from teammates Kevin Youkilis and Dave McCarty after blasting a three-run shot in the fifth inning. (AP/WWP)

"This is the beginning," manager Terry Francona said. "I think we're in good shape, but you don't write off what isn't supposed to be written off yet."

Bronson Arroyo (10-9) allowed only two runs in 6 1/3 strong innings to strengthen his bid for a spot in the postseason starting rotation. He gave the Sox five pitchers with 10 or more victories for the first time since 1979 (Dennis Eckersley, Bob Stanley, Mike Torrez, Steve Renko and Dick Drago).

The Sox wrapped up the final homestand of the season Sept. 26 believing their magic number was two to clinch a playoff spot, but further examination of the schedules of the three AL West contenders determined that chalking up win No. 94 would lock up a spot in the first round. With the West clubs playing each other, only one could possibly reach 94 victories and

that team would have to be the divisional winner.

"You never forget your first time, but this is a different team than last year," general manager Theo Epstein said. "We've had our own share of adversity. We were comatose for about three months, but the effort of these players pulling themselves out of it makes this really meaningful. We were 56-46 and a couple of games out of the wild card and things were in doubt, but these guys pulled themselves up by the bootstraps and persevered."

Two did end up being a key number last night. Thanks to Tampa starter Scott Kazmir's ill-advised decision to retaliate for a pair of hit batsmen by Arroyo, the dominating 20-year-old was ejected while working on a no-hitter in the fourth inning, opening the door for a Sox comeback.

Kazmir, who outpitched Pedro Martinez in a 5-2 win at Fenway Park on Sept. 14, held the Sox hitless for 3 1/3 innings before being tossed for hitting consecutive batters Ramirez and Kevin Millar. The Sox took advantage and erased a 2-0 deficit by pounding reliever Jorge Sosa for five runs in the fifth inning to take over for the duration of the evening. Damon belted a three-run homer to put the Sox ahead, and Ramirez followed later in the frame with a majestic blast off the roof of the cigar bar in deep center field.

Damon's 19th home run of the season established a new career high, while Ramirez' league-leading 43rd homer allowed him and David Ortiz to set a new club record for most homers by teammates (83). Ted Williams and Vern Stephens combined for 82 in 1949.

"We're solid top to bottom—bullpen, bench—we're definitely better than last year," Damon said. "Now everyone has the same goal: Break the curse."

BELOW: As Tim Wakefield (center left) watches Sox players David Ortiz (left), Ricky Gutierrez (center right) and Curtis Leskanic (far right) christen Manny Ramirez with champagne in the locker room after clinching the wild card playoff spot by beating the Tampa Bay Devil Rays 7-3. (AP/WWP)

AMERICAN
LEAGUE
DIVISION
SERIES

John Wilcox/Boston Herald

ONE DOWN,
ONE TO GO FOR SOX
IN ANAHEIM

BY JEFF HORRIGAN, BOSTON HERALD

Johnny Damon officially laid "Cowboy Up" to rest as the Red Sox' identifying slogan prior to the start of their American League Division Series at Angel Stadium.

	1 2 3	4 5 6	7 8 9	R	H	E
Boston	1 0 0	7 0 0	0 1 0	9	11	1
Anaheim	0 0 0	1 0 0	2 0 0	3	9	1

Boston	AB	R	H	RBI
Damon, CF	5	2	2	0
Bellhorn, 2B	4	0	0	0
Reese, 2B	0	0	0	0
Ramirez, LF	5	2	2	3
Ortiz, DH	3	1	1	1
Millar, 1B	4	1	2	2
Mientkiewicz, PR-1B	1	0	1	1
Varitek, C	5	1	1	0
Cabrera, SS	3	1	1	0
Mueller, 3B	4	0	0	0
Kapler, RF	5	1	1	0
Totals	39	9	11	7

Anaheim	AB	R	H	RBI
Figgins, 3B-2B	5	0	1	0
Erstad, 1B	4	1	3	1
Guerrero, RF	5	0	0	0
Anderson, CF	4	1	0	0
Glaus, DH	3	1	3	2
DaVanon, LF	3	0	0	0
Riggs, PH-LF	1	0	0	0
Molina, B., C	4	0	1	0
Eckstein, SS	4	0	1	0
Amezaga, 2B	1	0	0	0
McPherson, PH-3B	3	0	0	0
Totals	37	3	9	3

2B: Ramirez, Damon, Glaus 2; HR: Millar (1), Ramirez (1), Glaus (1), Erstad (1); SB: Damon, Figgins; E: Schilling, Figgins.

Boston	IP	H	R	ER	BB	SO
Schilling (W, 1-0)	6.2	9	3	2	2	4
Embree	0.1	0	0	0	0	0
Timlin	2.0	0	0	0	0	3

Anaheim	IP	H	R	ER	BB	SO
Washburn (L, 0-1)	3.1	5	7	3	3	3
Shields	1.2	1	1	1	1	2
Gregg	2.0	3	0	0	1	0
Ortiz	2.0	2	1	1	1	0

WP: Gregg; T: 3:04; Att: 44,608.

With cowboys about as plentiful in New England as surfers are in Nebraska, the Red Sox center fielder said there was a more appropriate way to capture the team's carefree attitude and individuality.

Idiots.

"We are not the cowboys anymore," Damon said. "We are just the idiots. ... We like to have fun and I think that's why this team is liked by so many people out there. We've got the long hair, we've got the corn rows, we've got guys acting like idiots, and I think the fans out there like it."

The timing of the pronouncement was fitting. With Pedro Martinez pitching and the Sox holding a 1-0 advantage in the best-of-five series following the 9-3 drubbing of the Anaheim Angels, even a genuine idiot can recognize that Boston is now in prime position to return to the AL Championship Series.

"We're definitely not going to be satisfied splitting here," said Damon, who went 2-for-5 with two runs scored in the victory. "We've got to go for the jugular and go home, 2-0."

The Sox used one of the largest offensive outbursts in the club's postseason history to

**ABOVE: Sox Kevin Millar fumbles the ball fielding a ground ball as he looks to throw to first.
(David Goldman/Boston Herald)**

" **We're definitely not going to be satisfied splitting here. We've got to go for the jugular and go home, 2-0.** "

—Johnny Damon

halt the momentum of the surging Angels. By jumping on Anaheim starter Jarrod Washburn for seven runs in the fourth inning, they built an 8-0 lead and kept the Rally Monkey locked in its cage.

Martinez lost his final four starts of the regular season but he's 9-1 lifetime against the Angels.

"Pedro's going to be ready," said David Ortiz, who drove in the Sox' first run of the game with a broken-bat single in the first inning. "I think the last game he pitched in the regular season was like a wake-up call."

Curt Schilling improved to 4-0 in his career against Anaheim, including three wins in as many starts this year. The right-hander allowed three runs on nine scattered hits in 6 2/3 innings

to win his ninth consecutive decision dating back to Aug. 9.

Schilling, who improved to 6-1 with a 1.74 ERA in postseason play, surrendered solo home runs to Troy Glaus and Darin Erstad. His seventh-inning throwing error on Garret Anderson's two-out bouncer to the right side of the mound allowed Anaheim to tack on an unearned run.

"I don't think there is a carryover," Schilling said of the effect of his win. "It's a tough place for us to win, but we have got Pedro going and I am pretty excited about that thought."

Washburn fell behind in the first inning and never caught up. Manny Ramirez banged a two-out double down the left field line and Ortiz followed with his RBI single to right.

BELOW: Sox catcher Jason Varitek slides to home plate as Anaheim catcher Bengie Molina loses a wild throw. (David Goldman/Boston Herald)

ABOVE: Manny Ramirez hits a three-run homer in the fourth inning at Angel Stadium. (David Goldman/Boston Herald)

The score remained 1-0 until the fourth, when the Sox exploded for seven runs, equaling their largest single-inning output ever in the postseason. It was last done in Game 3 of the 1999 ALDS against Cleveland. Prior to that, the Sox had scored six runs in a frame in the fifth game of the 1903 World Series at Pittsburgh and Game 1 of the 1975 World Series against Cincinnati.

Kevin Millar started the rally by belting a Washburn changeup into the left field seats for a two-run homer. With one out and the bases loaded, Damon hit a two-hopper to third baseman Chone Figgins, who threw wildly past catcher Bengie Molina in an attempt for a force at the plate. Two runs scored on the error. Two batters later, Ramirez delivered a three-run clout over the center field fence.

MARTINEZ, SOX
PROVE TWO GOOD
FOR ANGELS

BY JEFF HORRIGAN, BOSTON HERALD

Some of Pedro Martinez' teammates theorized that one of the reasons the three-time Cy Young Award winner stumbled at the finish of the regular season might have been due to some gamesmanship on his part.

The erstwhile Red Sox ace went 0-4 with a 7.72 ERA in his final four appearances, marking the first time he'd ever dropped four starts in a row in a single season. The fact that Martinez could still blow away hitters with overpowering fastballs in pressure situations, however, led some to believe that he simply may have been conserving his energy for the postseason, while lulling possible October opponents into complacency.

If Martinez was indeed playin' possum in September, it was appropriate he helped put the Anaheim Angels on the verge of becoming road-kill by pitching seven strong innings last night in an 8-3 victory at Angel Stadium that gave the Sox a commanding, 2-0 lead in the best-of-five AL Division Series.

In his first postseason appearance since squandering a three-run lead in Game 7 of the 2003 AL Championship Series, Martinez allowed only three runs on six hits, while striking out six batters. Keith Foulke preserved the lead over the final 1 1/3 innings to record the save.

	1	2	3		4	5	6		7	8	9		R	H	E
Boston	0	1	0		0	0	2		1	0	4		8	12	0
Anaheim	0	1	0		0	2	0		0	0	0		3	7	0

Boston	AB	R	H	RBI
Damon, CF	5	1	2	0
Bellhorn, 2B	3	0	1	0
Reese, 2B	0	0	0	0
Ramirez, LF	3	1	1	2
Ortiz, DH	2	1	1	0
Nixon, RF	5	0	1	1
Kapler, PR-RF	0	1	0	0
Millar, 1B	3	1	1	0
Mientkiewicz, 1B	2	0	1	0
Varitek, C	3	2	1	2
Cabrera, SS	5	0	1	3
Mueller, 3B	3	1	2	0
Roberts, PR	0	0	0	0
Youkilis, 3B	2	0	0	0
Totals	36	8	12	8

Anaheim	AB	R	H	RBI
Figgins, 2B	4	0	0	0
Erstad, 1B	3	0	1	0
Guerrero, RF	3	0	1	2
Anderson, CF	4	0	0	0
Glaus, DH	3	1	0	0
DaVanon, LF	4	0	2	0
McPherson, 3B	4	0	1	1
Molina, J., C	2	1	1	0
Kotchman, PH	1	0	0	0
Molina, B., C	0	0	0	0
Pride, PH	1	0	0	0
Eckstein, SS	3	1	1	0
Totals	32	3	7	3

2B: Ramirez, Cabrera; HR: Varitek (1); SB: Damon.

Boston	IP	H	R	ER	BB	SO
Martinez, P (W, 1-0)	7.0	6	3	3	2	6
Timlin	0.1	1	0	0	0	1
Myers	0.1	0	0	0	0	1
Foulke (S, 1)	1.1	0	0	0	0	2

Anaheim	IP	H	R	ER	BB	SO
Colon	6.0	7	3	3	3	3
Rodriguez (L, 0-1)	2.0	2	1	1	2	2
Donnelly	1.0	3	4	4	2	0

WP: Rodriguez 2, Donnelly; HBP: Erstad (by Martinez, P), Varitek (by Rodriguez).'
T: 3:48; Att: 45,118.

ABOVE: Anaheim's David Eckstein jumps over Sox David Ortiz to tag him out at second in the sixth inning. (David Goldman/Boston Herald)

"I'm really happy to go back to where I wanted to be and do the things I wanted to do," Martinez said. "Thank God I turned it around."

The Sox rallied from a 3-1 deficit after five innings and tied it in the sixth on Jason Varitek's two-run homer off Bartolo Colon before pulling ahead in the seventh against Francisco Rodriguez on Manny Ramirez' sacrifice fly. The Sox blew open the 4-3 game in the ninth with four runs off Brendan Donnelly. Orlando Cabrera had the key blow with a three-run double.

The 2-0 lead is the fourth in franchise history and the first since winning the first two games of the 1986 World Series at Shea Stadium. The Sox won the 1916 Series vs. Brooklyn and 1975 ALCS against Oakland after taking 2-0 leads.

LEFT: Pedro Martinez pitched seven strong innings, as the Sox won their second straight in Anaheim. (David Goldman/Boston Herald)

"We showed up to win, but you know [the Angels] feel good when they get to their bullpen," manager Terry Francona said. "Not only did we take the lead [against the bullpen], we tacked on. This bullpen was invincible. To get to them was huge."

The Sox had Colon on the ropes early. Damon and Mark Bellhorn opened the game with consecutive singles and David Ortiz drew a one-out walk to load them up but Boston marooned all three runners.

The Sox loaded the bases again with two outs in the second on a pair of singles and a

walk, but this time Ramirez drew a base on balls to force in Bill Mueller with the game's first run. A Bellhorn blunder, however, derailed the rally when he was picked off second by catcher Jose Molina.

Colon's escape buoyed his teammates, who immediately tied the game in the bottom of the second. Martinez walked leadoff batter Troy Glaus, who scored on successive singles by Jeff DaVanon and Dallas McPherson.

The score remained tied until the fifth, when Martinez surrendered a pair of runs that allowed the Angels to pull ahead for the first time in the series. Miscommunication between Cabrera and Ramirez allowed Molina's leadoff pop to drop in shallow left field for a single. After fouling off a pair of sacrifice bunt attempts, Eckstein poked a single to center and Martinez loaded the bases by hitting Darin Erstad on the left knee with a cut-fastball.

Vladimir Guerrero, who had been 0-for-6 in the series, then broke the tie by lining a two-run single to right-center field.

"There were some situations tonight where if something didn't go our way, we could lose that game," Francona said. "[Martinez] gave everything he had to do what he did."

BELOW: Jason Varitek hits a two-run homer in the sixth inning to tie the game. (David Goldman/Boston Herald)

ORTIZ BLAST OUTS ANGELS; WHO'S NEXT?

BY JEFF HORRIGAN, BOSTON HERALD

	1 2 3	4 5 6	7 8 9	10	R	H	E
Anaheim	0 0 0	1 0 0	5 0 0	0	6	8	2
Boston	0 0 2	3 1 0	0 0 0	2	8	12	0

Anaheim	AB	R	H	RBI
Figgins, 2B-3B	5	0	1	0
Erstad, 1B	3	1	1	1
Guerrero, RF	4	1	1	4
Anderson, CF	5	0	2	0
Glaus, DH	5	1	1	1
DaVanon, LF	3	1	0	0
Molina, B., C	2	0	0	0
Kotchman, PH	0	0	0	0
Molina, J., PH-C	1	1	0	0
McPherson, 3B	2	0	0	0
Riggs, PH	0	0	0	0
Pride, PH	1	0	0	0
Amezaga, 2B	1	0	0	0
Eckstein, SS	5	1	2	0
Totals	37	6	8	6

Boston	AB	R	H	RBI
Damon, CF	5	1	3	0
Bellhorn, 2B	4	2	0	0
Reese, PR	0	1	0	0
Ramirez, LF	5	0	2	2
Ortiz, DH	6	2	4	3
Nixon, RF	3	0	1	1
Millar, 1B	3	1	0	2
Mientkiewicz, 1B	1	0	0	0
Varitek, C	4	0	0	0
Cabrera, SS	5	0	0	0
Mueller, 3B	5	2	2	0
Totals	41	8	12	8

2B: Erstad, Ortiz 2; HR: Glaus (2), Guerrero (1), Ortiz (1); SB: Damon; E: Figgins, Eckstein.

Anaheim	IP	H	R	ER	BB	SO
Escobar	3.1	5	5	3	5	4
Shields	1.1	4	1	1	1	1
Donnelly	2.1	0	0	0	0	5
Rodriguez (L, 0-2)	2.2	2	1	1	1	3
Washburn	0.0	1	1	1	0	0

Boston	IP	H	R	ER	BB	SO
Arroyo	6.0	3	2	2	2	7
Myers	0.0	0	1	1	1	0
Timlin	0.2	2	3	3	1	1
Embree	0.2	0	0	0	1	0
Foulke	1.2	2	0	0	1	3
Lowe (W, 1-0)	1.0	1	0	0	1	0

HBP: Figgins (by Arroyo); T: 4:11; Att: 35,547.

For decades, the common refrain around Fenway Park for generations of Red Sox fans has been: "Here we go again."

Over the past two years, however, David Ortiz has put a welcome spin on it, converting the all-too-familiar regret to a euphoric: "There it goes again!"

The slugger, who has been the undisputed king of the game-winning hit since virtually the day he arrived in Boston, came through again last night by belting a walkoff, two-run home run off Jarrod Washburn to send the Sox to an 8-6, 10-inning victory and a three-game sweep of the Anaheim Angels in the American League Division Series.

Ortiz, who hit three game-winning homers during the regular season, greeted reliever Washburn by pounding his first-pitch slider over the Green Monster to wrap up the best-of-five series. The Sox will wait at least one more day to find out if they will be playing the New York Yankees or Minnesota Twins for the AL pennant. The series will begin in either the Bronx or Minneapolis Oct. 12.

"We went through a lot of this last year but it never gets old," general manager Theo Epstein said of the dramatics. "The guy never ceases to amaze me. In a spot like that, he's the guy you want at the plate."

The sweep was Boston's first in a postseason series since the 1975 ALCS vs. Oakland and it marked the Sox' first series-clincher at Fenway since the 1986 ALCS vs. the Angels. Ortiz joined Carlton Fisk (Game 6, 1975 World Series) and Trot Nixon (Game 3, 2003 ALDS) as the only players in club history to hit walk-off, postseason homers.

The Sox squandered a 6-1 lead and a marvelous pitching performance by starter Bronson Arroyo and allowed the Angels to tie the score at 6-6 in the seventh on Vladimir Guerrero's opposite-field grand slam off Mike Timlin. Relievers Keith Foulke and Derek Lowe walked a tightrope to hold it there and allow Ortiz to win it.

Johnny Damon started the game-winning rally by lining a Francisco Rodriguez pitch to left field for a base hit. Mark Bellhorn attempted to sacrifice him into scoring position, but bunted the ball too hard to third baseman

BELOW: David Ortiz sent the Sox to the ALCS for the second consecutive season with an extra-inning walkoff home run. (Michael Seamans/Boston Herald)

ABOVE: Bronson Arroyo pitched well enough to win, but a late Angels rally against the Sox' bullpen forced the game to extra innings. (John Wilcox/Boston Herald)

Chone Figgins, who threw to second base for the force on Damon. Rodriguez struck out Manny Ramirez looking for the second out and Anaheim manager Mike Scioscia responded by making a move that may haunt him forever.

He called on lefty Washburn, the losing pitcher in Game 1, to face left-handed hitter Ortiz.

"I was sitting next to Manny and I joked, 'Nice of you to leave the RBI out there for him,'" Timlin said. "Manny said, 'Don't worry, he hasn't hit a home run in about four days. He's due to hit one.' I couldn't believe it."

Ortiz, who donned swimming goggles in the clubhouse afterward to keep the endless flow of celebratory champagne out of his eyes, had barely crossed the plate when he began looking ahead.

"This is good for the pitching staff," he said. "Now they can take some time off and get some strength back in their arms. It will be good for us."

Arroyo allowed only three hits and struck out seven batters in six-plus innings and departed with a seemingly comfortable 6-1 lead after walking Jeff DaVanon to open the seventh. Mike Myers walked the only batter he faced (Jose Molina) before making way for Timlin, who loaded the bases on a walk and a single. The veteran right-hander forced in one run by walking Darin Erstad before leaving a fastball too far over the plate to Guerrero, who pounded it into the Boston bullpen for the Angels' first ever postseason grand slam, stunning the capacity crowd of 35,547.

"I put us in a hole, and [Ortiz] got us out," Timlin said.

ABOVE: Pokey Reese is mobbed at home plate as he is welcomed home after Ortiz' series-clinching blast. (Stuart Cahill/Boston Herald)

"I was sitting next to Manny and I joked, 'Nice of you to leave the RBI out there for him.' Manny said, 'Don't worry, he hasn't hit a home run in about four days. He's due to hit one.' I couldn't believe it."

—Mike Timlin

AMERICAN LEAGUE CHAMPIONSHIP SERIES

SCHILLING DIGS HOLE
SOX CAN'T ESCAPE

BY JEFF HORRIGAN, BOSTON HERALD

Through six innings last night, it appeared that the New York Yankees were going to adopt Pedro Martinez' teammates and become their proverbial daddy, as well.

When all was said and done at Yankee Stadium, however, the Yankees may have claimed a 10-7 victory in Game 1 of the American League Championship Series, but they learned

	1 2 3	4 5 6	7 8 9	R	H	E
Boston	0 0 0	0 0 0	5 2 0	7	10	0
NY Yankees	2 0 4	0 0 2	0 2 X	10	14	0

Boston	AB	R	H	RBI
Damon, CF	4	0	0	0
Bellhorn, 2B	4	1	1	0
Ramirez, LF	4	1	1	0
Ortiz, DH	4	1	2	2
Millar, 1B	4	1	1	2
Nixon, RF	4	1	1	1
Varitek, C	4	1	2	2
Cabrera, SS	4	0	1	0
Mueller, 3B	4	1	1	0
Totals	**36**	**7**	**10**	**7**

NY Yankees	AB	R	H	RBI
Jeter, SS	4	1	2	0
Rodriguez, 3B	5	2	2	0
Sheffield, RF	4	4	3	0
Matsui, LF	5	2	3	5
Williams, CF	5	0	2	3
Posada, C	3	0	0	1
Olerud, 1B	3	0	1	0
Cairo, 2B	4	0	1	0
Lofton, DH	3	1	1	1
Totals	**36**	**10**	**14**	**10**

2B: Bellhorn, Millar, Sheffield 2, Matsui 2, Williams; 3B: Ortiz; HR: Varitek (1), Lofton (1).

Boston	IP	H	R	ER	BB	SO
Schilling (L, 0-1)	3.0	6	6	6	2	1
Leskanic	1.0	0	0	0	2	1
Mendoza	1.0	1	0	0	0	0
Wakefield	1.0	3	2	2	0	1
Embree	1.0	1	0	0	0	0
Timlin	0.2	3	2	2	0	0
Foulke	0.1	0	0	0	0	0

NY Yankees	IP	H	R	ER	BB	SO
Mussina (W, 1-0)	6.2	4	4	4	0	8
Sturtze	0.1	1	1	1	0	1
Gordon	0.2	3	2	2	0	0
Rivera (S, 1)	1.1	2	0	0	0	1

HBP: Posada (by Mendoza); T: 3:20; Att: 56,135.

that they're going to have to round up an unruly bunch of runaways first if they hope to return to the World Series.

On the verge of being humiliated after Curt Schilling's worst start in a Boston uniform, the Red Sox fought back from an 8-0 deficit and climbed to within a run of the Yankees, only to fall short.

Martinez will try to even the series, when he squares off against New York's Jon Lieber.

"To be down, 8-0, and make it 8-7 shows a lot about our character," Kevin Millar said. "We're going to bounce back and give them another fight."

Clearly hampered by an injured right ankle, Schilling surrendered six runs in only three innings and departed trailing, 6-0. Limited by ankle tendinitis since Sept. 21, the right-hander had difficulty driving off the mound, which led to a laggard fastball and poor pitch location, not to mention a humbling outing before a national audience. He surrendered six hits and two walks while striking out only one batter, marking the first time since May 28, 1998, that Schilling finished with more walks than whiffs.

"I've been looking forward to this almost a year, so it was incredibly disappointing," Schilling said. "I just couldn't make [the ankle] work. I couldn't get anything on the ball and I couldn't command my pitches."

Schilling, who was undefeated (6-0) in his nine previous postseason starts dating back to a Game 1 loss in the 1993 World Series, vowed that he wouldn't pitch again in the series unless he felt he could improve.

"If I can't go out there with something better than I had, I'm not going out there," he said. "It's not about me. This is about something bigger."

Opposing starter Mike Mussina mesmerized the Sox for six innings, only to see his perfect game bid ended by a five-run rally in the seventh. Mussina, who lost Game 1 of the 2003 ALCS, was charged with four runs in 6 2/3 innings, while Jason Varitek belted a two-run home run off reliever Tanyon Sturtze.

"During the first six innings, [Mussina] kind of put on a clinic," Sox manager Terry Francona said. "He was throwing different speeds, different pitches, up, down, nothing was over the middle of the plate. Everything was on the black."

The Sox pulled to within 8-7 against Tom Gordon in the eighth on David Ortiz' two-out triple. But Mariano Rivera, who returned from attending to a family tragedy in Panama after the game had begun, got Millar to pop out to strand the potential tying run at third base.

The Sox' momentum, however, slipped away in the bottom of the eighth when New York added a pair of insurance runs on Bernie Williams' two-run double off Mike Timlin. Rivera recorded his 31st career postseason save, but the Sox didn't make it easy on him. Singles by Varitek and Orlando Cabrera brought the tying run to the plate once again, but Bill Mueller bounced into a game-ending double play.

"We won the first game last year and look what happened," said Johnny Damon, who went 0-for-4 with four strikeouts. "There's no quit here, but hopefully we can get our offense started a little earlier [in Game 2]."

Schilling gave up two runs in the first inning and four more in the third, leading to his earliest exit under routine conditions in 7 1/2 years. He made a two-inning start in San Diego for the Arizona Diamondbacks on July 18, 2001, when an electrical transformer exploded at Qualcomm Stadium, leaving part of the park in darkness. Prior to that, Schilling's shortest outing was May 22, 1997, when he was hammered for nine runs in only 2 2/3 innings in the Philadelphia Phillies' 10-3 loss to the New York Mets at Veterans Stadium.

The start was the Sox' shortest in a postseason game since Bret Saberhagen lasted only 2 2/3 innings in an 11-1 thumping against the Cleveland Indians in Game 2 of the 1999 ALDS.

BELOW: Curt Schilling shows his frustration with the shortest postseason outing of his career. (Matthew West/Boston Herald)

SILENT BATS
STRAND MARTINEZ
IN BRONX

BY JEFF HORRIGAN, BOSTON HERALD

Pedro Martinez' performance in the second game of the American League Championship Series showed it was no longer necessary for him to call the New York Yankees his daddy.

Despite turning in a quality start, however, he and the Red Sox are on the verge of having to say "uncle" to their bitter rivals after losing for the second consecutive night, 3-1, at Yankee Stadium.

Martinez had his most impressive fastball in years and surrendered only three runs on four hits in six innings while striking out seven batters, but he was no match for Jon Lieber. The New York right-hander allowed one run on three hits while striking out three in seven-plus innings to lead the Yankees to a 2-0 advantage in the best-of-seven series.

Since the advent of the seven-game League Championship Series in 1985, 13 of 15 teams that have taken a 2-0 lead have advanced to the World Series.

"We know we're in a hole, but even idiots know how to dig themselves out of a hole," said Johnny Damon, who is 0-for-8 in the series with five strikeouts.

After falling to New York, 6-4, at Fenway Park Sept. 24, a frustrated Martinez uttered the most memorable quote of the year: "What can I do but tip my hat and call the Yankees my daddy?"

The three-time Cy Young Award winner said he hoped he never had to face the Yankees again and expressed a desire to bury himself on

	1	2	3		4	5	6		7	8	9		R	H	E
Boston	0	0	0		0	0	0		0	1	0		1	5	0
NY Yankees	1	0	0		0	0	2		0	0	X		3	7	0

Boston		AB		R		H		RBI
Damon, CF		4		0		0		0
Bellhorn, 2B		4		0		0		0
Ramirez, LF		4		0		1		0
Ortiz, DH		3		0		1		0
Millar, 1B		4		0		0		0
Nixon, RF		3		1		1		0
Varitek, C		3		0		1		0
Cabrera, SS		3		0		1		1
Mueller, 3B		3		0		0		0
Totals		31		1		5		1

NY Yankees		AB		R		H		RBI
Jeter, SS		3		1		0		0
Rodriguez, 3B		4		0		1		0
Sheffield, RF		4		0		2		1
Matsui, LF		4		0		1		0
Williams, CF		4		0		0		0
Posada, C		2		1		1		0
Olerud, 1B		4		1		1		2
Cairo, 2B		2		0		0		0
Lofton, DH		4		0		1		0
Totals		31		3		7		3

2B: Varitek, Ramirez; HR: Olerud (1); SB: Jeter.

Boston	IP	H	R	ER	BB	SO
Martinez, P (L, 0-1)	6.0	4	3	3	4	7
Timlin	0.2	1	0	0	0	0
Embree	0.2	2	0	0	0	0
Foulke	0.2	0	0	0	1	1

NY Yankees	IP	H	R	ER	BB	SO
Lieber (W, 1-0)	7.0	3	1	1	1	3
Gordon	0.2	1	0	0	0	0
Rivera (S, 2)	1.1	1	0	0	0	3

HBP: Rodriguez (by Martinez, P), Cairo (by Foulke); T: 3:15; Att: 56,136.

the mound after blowing a 3-2 lead. The raucous capacity crowd didn't let Martinez forget the statements and taunted him with "Who's your daddy?" chants all night. With a little run support, however, he knows that he could have buried the Yanks.

"I can't do anything if we don't score runs," Martinez said. "I can only pitch. From there, it's up to them."

The Sox, who led the major leagues in runs for the second consecutive year, didn't score until the eighth inning, when Trot Nixon

ABOVE: Pedro Martinez looks on as John Olerud rounds the bases after a sixth-inning home run. (Matthew West/Boston Herald)

ended Lieber's evening with a leadoff single and eventually scored on a groundout. The Sox went 0-for-7 with runners in scoring position.

"Pedro pitched well enough to win that game," Jason Varitek said. "We just didn't do the job on the other end. We lost this game for him."

Rumors abounded prior to the game that Martinez may have been under the weather, but it must have been wishful thinking because he started the game with his best fastball of the year. He hit 94 mph with his first pitch and was up to 97 four batters in. The velocity is believed to be the highest for Martinez since just before he strained his right shoulder in June 2001. Unfortunately, it didn't slow down the Yankees, who scored in the first inning for the second consecutive night.

Martinez opened the inning by missing the mark with his first four pitches to Derek Jeter.

He then brushed the left hand of Alex Rodriguez with a 2-2 pitch, and Gary Sheffield followed by lining a poorly placed pitch to center field to drive in Jeter.

Martinez marooned two runners in the first and then again in the second, and held it at 1-0 until the sixth. Martinez walked Posada with one out, and John Olerud followed by turning on an up-and-in fastball and lining it into the right field seats for a two-run homer.

Lieber stunned the Sox on Sept. 18, when he held them hitless for six innings in the Bronx. The Sox hitters fell into a similar pattern by swinging early and often, allowing Lieber to breeze through the first six innings, allowing only one hit.

"They've pitched very effectively so far and when they've made mistakes, we haven't made them pay for it," manager Terry Francona said.

SOX HEART BROKEN
BY BRONX
BOMBSHELL

BY JEFF HORRIGAN, BOSTON HERALD

When author Stephen King decided to write a book on the 2004 Red Sox season, he anticipated it being a labor of love and a tribute from a lifelong fan to a team projected to make a run at ending an 86-year championship drought.

Predictably, it now appears that it's going to have a horrific ending.

After falling short in the first two games of the American League Championship Series to the New York Yankees in the Bronx, the Sox were ripped apart as viciously as one of Cujo's prey in a humiliating 19-8 loss at Fenway Park.

Bronson Arroyo and five relievers shared the role of "Firestarter" and surrendered 22 hits, including 13 for extra bases, resulting in the Yankees establishing a record for runs scored in an LCS game in the longest nine-inning game in postseason history, while taking a commanding 3-0 lead in the best-of-seven series.

It's too bad King (who was sitting in the second row) has already used the title *Misery*, because no team has come back from a 3-0 deficit to win a seven-game series in Major League Baseball history. Of the 25 previous teams to jump ahead 3-0, 20 have gone on to sweep the series in four games.

"It was definitely an ass-whupping," Johnny Damon said. "They're doing exactly what we thought we would be doing in this series. . . . We

	1	2	3	4	5	6	7	8	9	R	H	E
NY Yankees	3	0	3	5	2	0	4	0	2	19	22	1
Boston	0	4	2	0	0	0	2	0	0	8	15	0

NY Yankees	AB	R	H	RBI
Jeter, SS	4	2	1	0
Rodriguez, 3B	5	5	3	3
Sheffield, RF	5	3	4	4
Crosby, PR-RF	0	1	0	0
Matsui, LF	6	5	5	5
Williams, CF	6	1	4	3
Posada, C	5	1	2	1
Sierra, R., DH	6	0	2	2
Olerud, 1B	4	0	0	0
Clark, 1B	2	0	0	0
Cairo, 2B	4	1	1	0
Totals	47	19	22	18

Boston	AB	R	H	RBI
Damon, CF	5	1	1	1
Bellhorn, 2B	4	0	0	0
Ramirez, LF	4	0	1	0
Ortiz, DH	5	1	3	0
Varitek, C	3	3	2	2
Mirabelli, C	1	0	0	0
Nixon, RF	5	1	2	2
Millar, 1B	5	1	1	0
Mueller, 3B	4	1	2	0
Cabrera, SS	4	0	3	2
Totals	40	8	15	7

2B: Rodriguez 2, R. Sierra, Matsui 2, Sheffield, Williams, Posada, Mueller, Millar, Cabrera 2, Nixon; 3B: R. Sierra; HR: Matsui 2 (2), Rodriguez (1), Sheffield (1), Nixon (1), Varitek (1). E: Jeter.

NY Yankees	IP	H	R	ER	BB	SO
Brown	2.0	5	4	3	2	1
Vazquez (W, 1-0)	4.1	7	4	4	2	4
Quantrill	1.2	2	0	0	0	2
Gordon	1.0	1	0	0	0	1

Boston	IP	H	R	ER	BB	SO
Arroyo	2.0	6	6	6	2	0
Mendoza (L, 0-1)	1.0	1	1	1	0	1
Leskanic	0.1	2	3	3	1	0
Wakefield	3.1	5	5	5	2	1
Embree	0.1	3	2	2	0	0
Myers	2.0	5	2	2	2	3

WP: Brown, Gordon; Balk: Mendoza; HBP: Cairo (by Mendoza); T: 4:20; Att: 35,126.

felt we'd be up 3-0 right now, but those guys have found another switch."

The game had as many ups and downs as a King thriller in the early innings, with the teams surrendering three leads in the first 3 1/2 innings, but New York broke a 6-6 tie with a five-run rally in the fourth inning and never looked back. Gary Sheffield put the Yankees ahead for the duration of the interminable evening by walloping a three-run homer into the Green Monster seats off Curtis Leskanic.

The capacity crowd got so discouraged by the middle innings that it began throwing foul balls back onto the field rather than taking home a reminder of the debacle. Fenway is typically known as a stadium where loyal fans remain to the end but it turned into a "Dead Zone" after a significant portion filed out after the sixth inning.

Hideki Matsui went 5-for-6 with two home runs, five RBIs and five runs scored, while Sheffield went 4-for-5 with four RBIs and three runs. Alex Rodriguez had three hits, including a homer, knocked in three runs and scored five runs.

"At crunch time, to have a football score up there like that is definitely embarrassing," said Arroyo, who was hammered for six runs in two innings.

The Yankees wasted no time jumping out to a 3-0 lead in the first inning. Rodriguez followed Derek Jeter's leadoff walk by lashing a RBI double to the left field corner, and Matsui stepped up two batters later and hit a two-run homer into the visitors' bullpen.

Trot Nixon's two-run homer helped Boston score four runs in the second inning to take a 4-3 lead but it was short-lived. Rodriguez tied it leading off the third by blasting an Arroyo curveball onto Lansdowne Street. Ramiro Mendoza added to the destruction by balking in a run as the Yanks went ahead, 6-4.

The Sox tied the game in the bottom of the third on Orlando Cabrera's bases-loaded, two-run double.

New York instantly broke the tie by tallying five times in the fourth to surge ahead, and the rout was on.

"This is as big a hole as you could dig yourself in," Arroyo said.

LEFT: Bill Mueller is tagged out at the plate by Yankees catcher Jorge Posada. (Matthew West/Boston Herald)

PAPI, SOX SHOW 'EM WHO'S DADDY

BY JEFF HORRIGAN, BOSTON HERALD

The Red Sox evidently aren't quite ready to accept their new daddies.

Trailing by a run with only three outs remaining, the Sox rallied to tie the score in the bottom of ninth inning before David Ortiz belted his second walkoff home run of the postseason in the 12th to send them to an uplifting, 6-4, victory over the New York Yankees to stave off a sweep in the longest game in American League Championship Series history.

Ortiz clobbered a Paul Quantrill fastball into the visitors' bullpen to complete Boston's improbable comeback.

"Things can change in a moment," Ortiz said. "You never know what will happen. This team never gives up."

The Sox cut the Yankees' series lead to 3-1, keeping hope alive in New England that they can make history by becoming the first team in Major League Baseball to overcome a 3-0 deficit in a best-of-seven series.

"Our season was nearly over, but we get to live another day," Johnny Damon said.

The Yankees will try to prevent the series from returning to New York in Game 5 of the series at Fenway.

"You can't help but think that there's some momentum now," winning pitcher Curtis Leskanic said. "Our guys are pretty pumped right now and hopefully this sets the tone for [Game 5]."

	1 2 3	4 5 6	7 8 9	10 11 12	R	H	E
NY Yankees	0 0 2	0 0 2	0 0 0	0 0 0	4	12	1
Boston	0 0 0	0 3 0	0 0 1	0 0 2	6	8	0

NY Yankees	AB	R	H	RBI
Jeter, SS	4	1	1	0
Rodriguez, 3B	5	1	1	2
Sheffield, RF	5	0	0	0
Matsui, LF	5	1	2	0
Williams, CF	6	0	1	1
Posada, C	4	1	2	0
Sierra, R., DH	6	0	2	0
Clark, 1B	6	0	2	1
Cairo, 2B	4	0	1	0
Totals	45	4	12	4

Boston	AB	R	H	RBI
Damon, CF	5	1	0	0
Cabrera, SS	6	1	1	1
Ramirez, LF	3	1	2	0
Ortiz, DH	5	1	2	4
Varitek, C	5	0	0	0
Nixon, RF	5	0	0	0
Millar, 1B	2	0	1	0
Roberts, PR	0	1	0	0
Reese, 2B	1	0	0	0
Mueller, 3B	5	1	2	1
Bellhorn, 2B	2	0	0	0
Mientkiewicz, PH-1B	1	0	0	0
Totals	40	6	8	6

2B: Matsui; 3B: Matsui; HR: Rodriguez (2), Ortiz (1); SB: Roberts, Damon; E: Clark

NY Yankees	IP	H	R	ER	BB	SO
Hernandez	5.0	3	3	3	5	6
Sturtze	2.0	1	0	0	0	1
Rivera	2.0	2	1	1	2	2
Gordon	2.0	0	0	0	1	1
Quantrill (L, 0-1)	0.0	2	2	2	0	0

Boston	IP	H	R	ER	BB	SO
Lowe	5.1	6	3	3	0	3
Timlin	1.0	3	1	1	3	0
Foulke	2.2	0	0	0	2	3
Embree	1.2	2	0	0	1	0
Myers	0.0	0	0	0	1	0
Leskanic (W, 1-0)	1.1	1	0	0	0	1

WP: Timlin; T: 5:02; Att: 34,826.

The Sox trailed, 4-3, heading into the ninth after leaving the potential tying run at second base in the eighth. Rivera, who returned from a family tragedy in Panama to save the first two games of the series at Yankee Stadium, walked Kevin Millar to open the ninth, and pinch-runner Dave Roberts immediately stole second base. Bill Mueller followed with a hard single bounced up the middle that scored Roberts with the tying run.

A Tony Clark error and a Manny Ramirez walk loaded the bases with two outs, but Ortiz popped out to send the game into extra innings.

The Yankees threatened in the top of the 11th, but left the bases loaded when Leskanic got Bernie Williams to fly out. Leskanic left a runner at second base in the top of the 12th before the Sox won it in the bottom half of the inning.

> **Our season was nearly over, but we get to live another day.**
>
> —Johnny Damon

ABOVE: Dave Roberts scores to tie the game in the ninth inning. (Michael Seamans/Boston Herald)

Ramirez, who reached base safely in 5-of-6 plate appearances, slammed a leadoff single to left field before Ortiz lined a 2-1 fastball over right fielder Gary Sheffield and into the 'pen.

"If you look around this room, most guys might do that once, twice or three times in their career," Millar said. "[Ortiz] does it three or four times a year."

Sox starter Derek Lowe was charged with three runs on six hits in 5 1/3, innings and he held the Yankees scoreless in the first inning for the first time in the series. The right-hander served up a mammoth two-run homer to Alex Rodriguez in the third inning, giving New York a 2-0 lead.

New York starting pitcher Orlando Hernandez, meanwhile, was solid until the fifth, when Boston rallied for three runs to take the lead, 3-2. Hernandez had himself to blame for his lost lead. He walked three in the inning and gave up all the runs with two outs on singles by Orlando Cabrera and Ortiz (two RBIs), providing Boston only its second lead of the series.

The advantage was short-lived. Francona replaced Lowe after Hideki Matsui lined a one-out triple to the center field triangle in the sixth, and the lead quickly slipped away under Mike Timlin, who allowed three infield hits and two walks. Williams' slow chopper to the left side allowed Matsui to score the tying run and diving second baseman Mark Bellhorn could only knock down Clark's two-out two-hopper to the right side, which permitted Jorge Posada to score and push the Yankees ahead, 4-3.

BELOW: David Ortiz gave the Sox life after hitting the game-winning home run in the 12th inning. (David Goldman/Boston Herald)

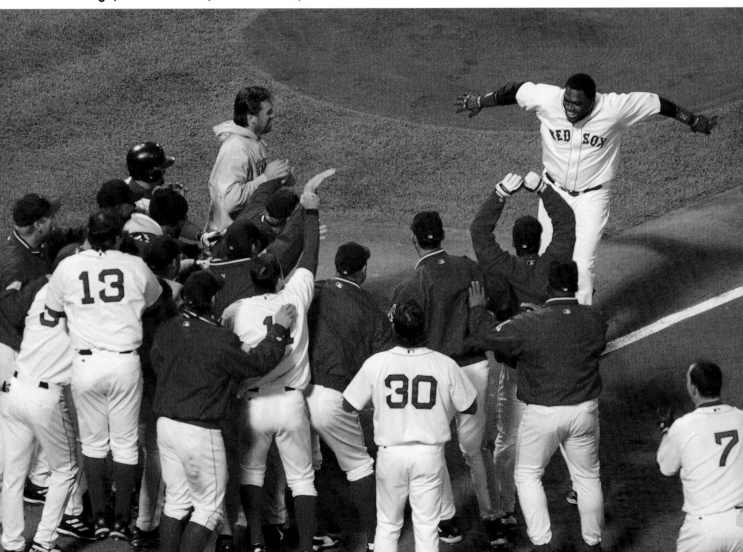

ORTIZ, SOX RALLY TO FIGHT ANOTHER DAY

BY JEFF HORRIGAN, BOSTON HERALD

	1 2 3	4 5 6	7 8 9	10 11 12	13 14	R	H	E
NY Yankees	0 1 0	0 0 3	0 0 0	0 0 0	0 0	4	12	1
Boston	2 0 0	0 0 0	0 2 0	0 0 0	0 1	5	13	1

NY Yankees	AB	R	H	RBI
Jeter, SS	7	0	1	3
Rodriguez, 3B	4	0	0	0
Sheffield, RF	4	0	0	0
Matsui, LF	7	0	1	0
Williams, CF	7	1	2	1
Posada, C	6	1	2	0
Sierra, R., DH	5	1	3	0
Clark, 1B	7	0	1	0
Cairo, 2B	6	1	2	0
Totals	53	4	12	4

Boston	AB	R	H	RBI
Damon, CF	6	1	1	0
Cabrera, SS	6	1	2	0
Ramirez, LF	6	0	2	0
Ortiz, DH	6	2	3	3
Millar, 1B	2	0	0	0
Roberts, PR	0	1	0	0
Mientkiewicz, 1B	2	0	1	0
Nixon, RF	4	0	1	0
Kapler, PR-RF	2	0	0	0
Varitek, C	4	0	0	2
Mueller, 3B	6	0	1	0
Bellhorn, 2B	6	0	2	0
Totals	50	5	13	5

2B: Jeter, Cairo, Clark, Bellhorn, Mientkiewicz; HR: Williams (1), Ortiz (2).
SF: Varitek; E: Jeter, Ramirez

NY Yankees	IP	H	R	ER	BB	SO
Mussina	6.0	6	2	2	2	7
Sturtze	0.1	0	0	0	1	0
Gordon	0.2	2	2	2	1	0
Rivera	2.0	1	0	0	0	1
Heredia	0.1	1	0	0	0	1
Quantrill	1.0	2	0	0	0	0
Loaiza (L, 0-1)	3.1	1	1	1	3	3

Boston	IP	H	R	ER	BB	SO
Martinez, P	6.0	7	4	4	5	6
Timlin	1.2	2	0	0	1	1
Foulke	1.1	1	0	0	1	0
Arroyo	1.0	0	0	0	0	2
Myers	0.1	0	0	0	0	1
Embree	0.2	1	0	0	0	2
Wakefield (W, 1-0)	3.0	1	0	0	1	4

HBP: Cairo (by Martinez, P), Rodriguez (by Martinez, P); T: 5:49; Att: 35,120.

The official crowd at Fenway Park was a capacity 35,120, but as the years pass, the number of people who claim to have attended the Red Sox' 5-4, 14-inning victory against the New York Yankees in Game 5 of the American League Championship Series undoubtedly will swell.

Less than 22 hours after keeping the Sox' hopes alive by belting a walkoff, two-run home run in the 12th inning of Game 4, David Ortiz repeated the feat when he finished the longest game in postseason history by lining a two-out RBI single in the 14th.

"I might be in some sort of a haze, but I think that has to be the greatest game that's ever been played," Sox general manager Theo Epstein said. "I'd like to hear other nominations because that was just incredible."

Ortiz, who repeatedly spits on the Jamesian notion that there is no such thing as a clutch player, fouled off five two-strike pitches from Esteban Loaiza before fisting the 10th pitch of the at-bat into center field to score Johnny Damon from second base. Damon, who is 2-for-24 in the series, drew a one-out walk and moved into scoring position on Manny Ramirez' two-out walk.

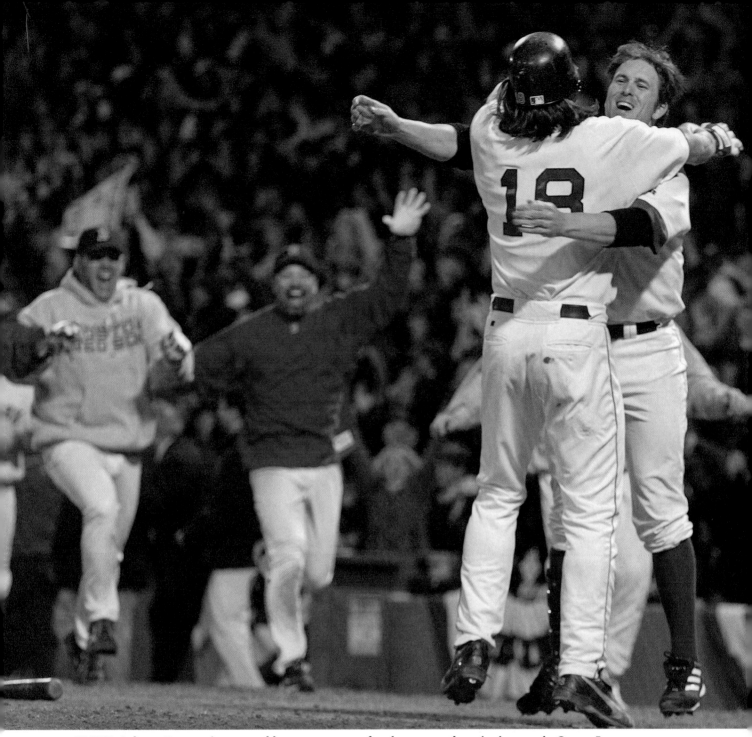

ABOVE: Johnny Damon is greeted by teammates after he scores the winning run in Game 5. (Nancy Lane/Boston Herald)

"The way he's going, there might be a nice monument for him around here some day," Damon said of Ortiz.

Ortiz came within feet of ending the game with another walkoff homer, but he pulled a Loaiza fastball foul moments before lining the slider to center.

"David's got a habit of coming through, and that was one of the best at-bats I've ever seen," Epstein said. "Loaiza was throwing nuclear stuff and to foul those balls off and then get that hit to center field was unbelievable."

The Sox cut the Yankees' series lead to 3-2, keeping hope alive that they can become the first team in Major League Baseball history to over-

BELOW: Mark Bellhorn jumps over Yankee Alex Rodriguez after getting him out at second and completing the double play. (David Goldman/Boston Herald)

come a 3-0 deficit and win a seven-game series. Both teams twice left the potential winning run in scoring position in extra innings before the Sox won it in the 14th, five hours and 49 minutes after the game's first pitch.

"The first three games were an aberration of what this team is all about," Epstein said. "This team wasn't ready to go home."

The Sox had seven winning streaks of at least four games this season, but they haven't defeated the Yankees four times in four days since June 4-7, 1990. They did, however, defeat New York in four consecutive games earlier this year on April 19 at Fenway and April 23-25 in the Bronx.

The Yanks, who sent the Sox to their seventh straight second-place finish in the AL East, need to win Game 6 or Game 7 to win their 40th pennant and earn a trip to the World Series against either Houston or St. Louis.

Derek Jeter's three-run double off Pedro Martinez with two outs in the sixth inning erased the Sox' 2-1 lead and pushed New York ahead, 4-2, but the Sox were unfazed.

Similar to the way they erased a 4-3 lead in the ninth inning of Game 4, the Sox did away with New York's two-run advantage in the eighth. Ortiz began the comeback by blasting a leadoff homer off Tom Gordon over the Green Monster. Kevin Millar drew a walk, and Trot Nixon followed with a hit-and-run single up the middle that moved pinch-runner Dave Roberts to third.

Yankees manager Joe Torre then called on closer Mariano Rivera, who failed to nail down the win in Game 4, and the stopper blew another save by surrendering a game-tying sacrifice fly to Jason Varitek.

"We've been treating these [last two] games like one-game playoffs," Varitek said. "That's the way this team has focused."

Impending free agent Martinez, who might have made his final appearance at Fenway in a home uniform, allowed a run in the first five frames before losing his mastery—and a 2-1 lead—in the sixth on Jeter's clutch double.

"**I might be in some sort of a haze, but I think that has to be the greatest game that's ever been played. I'd like to hear other nominations because that was just incredible.**"

—Theo Epstein

RIGHT: David Ortiz makes it two games in a row with walk-off extra-inning hit. (Michael Seamans/Boston Herald)

DH
34

DAVID ORTIZ

BY KAREN GUREGIAN

Just as the Red Sox were left trying to figure a way to keep Hideki Matsui from burying them with his bat after the first three games, the Bronx Bombers also had a puzzle to solve if they had any hope of moving onto the World Series and eliminating the Sox once and for all.

Simply put, David Ortiz has been the bane of George Steinbrenner's existence. He has absolutely croaked the Yankees during the American League Championship Series.

As Pedro Martinez piped in after Game 5: "The Yankees have to think about who is their Papi?"

Ortiz has pretty much owned everyone who has taken the ball from Joe Torre in this series. He beat the Yanks in Game 4 with a walkoff homer off Paul Quantrill. Then in Game 5, he homered off Tom Gordon to draw the Red Sox within a run in the eighth inning, then ended the game six innings later with an RBI bloop single off Esteban Loiaza.

Gordon was asked prior to Game 6 if the Yankees had to now devise a special plan to try and eliminate Ortiz.

"Well, he's been the guy for them," Gordon said. "He's definitely hot."

In Game 5, Ortiz cranked a Gordon fastball, which was supposed to be down and away, up and over the Green Monster seats.

In all, heading into Game 6, the Sox' slugger was batting .478 (11-for-23) with 19 total bases, two home runs and nine of Boston's 26 RBIs in the series.

"He's so strong. He can hit any pitch out of the ballpark at any given time," Gordon said. "You just have to stay aggressive on him, first

pitch to last pitch. He doesn't get himself out. He's tough."

Tough, to the point of legend status. Ortiz' ability to hit in the clutch, to deliver one big blow after another, one game-winning bomb after another, has left the Pinstripes both in awe, and in a state.

"He's been a handful, there's no question," Yankees manager Joe Torre said. "You saw he had a chance to be a good hitter when he was in Minnesota, but he's gotten so much stronger and so much more confident. He's certainly a force."

Gordon believes Ortiz has been helped by having good hitters around him, namely Manny Ramirez.

"Manny one of best pure hitters in all of baseball. He never gives himself away. And Ortiz is starting to show that," Gordon said. "I think Manny has helped him. Now you got two Manny Ramirezes; one on the right, one on the left. You see Manny, then you see a guy who is absolutely identical to him, and he's a left-hander.

"You can't think he's looking fastball, and throw him a breaking ball," Gordon went on. "You can't think he's looking for a breaking ball, and throw him a fastball. You just can't find a set pattern for those guys."

Ortiz reminds Gordon of former Sox teammate Mo Vaughn, only Ortiz is an even scarier proposition at the plate.

"He's a left-handed Manny Ramirez, with a Mo Vaughn swing," Gordon said.

He's also trouble.

SOX ARE BACK
AND BETTER
THAN EVER

BY JEFF HORRIGAN, BOSTON HERALD

Brace yourself, New England, because here we go again.

All but written off just a matter of days ago, the Red Sox are now on the verge of rewriting baseball history, thanks to the heroic effort of Curt Schilling at Yankee Stadium.

	1	2	3		4	5	6		7	8	9		R	H	E
Boston	0	0	0		4	0	0		0	0	0		4	11	0
NY Yankees	0	0	0		0	0	0		1	1	0		2	6	0

Boston	AB	R	H	RBI
Damon, CF	5	0	1	0
Mueller, 3B	4	0	0	0
Ramirez, LF	4	0	1	0
Ortiz, DH	4	0	0	0
Nixon, RF	3	0	0	0
Kapler, PH-RF	1	0	1	0
Millar, 1B	4	1	2	0
Mientkiewicz, 1B	0	0	0	0
Varitek, C	4	1	3	1
Cabrera, SS	4	1	2	0
Bellhorn, 2B	3	1	1	3
Reese, PR-2B	0	0	0	0
Totals	36	4	11	4

NY Yankees	AB	R	H	RBI
Jeter, SS	4	0	1	1
Rodriguez, 3B	4	0	1	0
Sheffield, RF	4	0	1	0
Matsui, LF	3	0	0	0
Williams, CF	4	1	1	1
Posada, C	4	0	0	0
Sierra, R., DH	3	0	0	0
Clark, 1B	4	0	0	0
Cairo, 2B	3	1	2	0
Totals	33	2	6	2

2B: Millar, Cairo 2; HR: Bellhorn (1), Williams (2); SB: Cabrera.

Boston	IP	H	R	ER	BB	SO
Schilling (W, 1-1)	7.0	4	1	1	0	4
Arroyo	1.0	2	1	1	0	1
Foulke (S, 1)	1.0	0	0	0	2	2

NY Yankees	IP	H	R	ER	BB	SO
Lieber (L, 1-1)	7.1	9	4	4	0	2
Heredia	0.1	0	0	0	0	0
Quantrill	0.2	2	0	0	0	0
Sturtze	0.2	0	0	0	1	0

WP: Lieber; HBP: Mueller (by Lieber); T: 3:50; Att: 56,128.

The major league wins leader during the regular season, who was thought to be done for the postseason after suffering a serious ankle injury, provided just the kick the Sox needed after three exhausting days at Fenway Park, sending them to a 4-2 victory over the New York Yankees to even the American League Championship Series at three wins apiece and forcing a decisive Game 7.

Keith Foulke came on and nailed down the win in the ninth inning but not without plenty of drama. He sandwiched two walks around two outs before whiffing former Sox Tony Clark on a 3-2 fastball.

A win in Game 7 would make the Sox the first team in baseball to overcome a 3-0 deficit to win a seven-game series. No club had ever forced a Game 7 after falling behind 3-0.

Schilling, who will require offseason surgery to repair a dislocated peroneal tendon in his right ankle, returned to the mound for the first time since getting hammered in Game 1 and held the Yankees to only one run on four hits in seven dominating innings. He struck out four, walked none and held New York hitless in four at-bats with runners in scoring position.

ABOVE: Alex Rodriguez whipped up a storm of controversy when he slapped the ball out of Bronson Arroyo's glove in the eighth inning of Game 6. (Nancy Lane/Boston Herald)

"That was definitely inspiring," Johnny Damon said. "We know Curt had someone looking down on him to get through seven strong innings like that."

Schilling's only slip-up occurred in the seventh, when Bernie Williams belted a solo, upper-deck home run, but it only dented a 4-0 lead provided by Boston's four-run rally in the fourth inning. Mark Bellhorn, who had Fenway fans turn on him due to his struggles during the epic 15 hours, 11 minutes of ball over the previous three days, provided the key blow with a three-run homer off Jon Lieber.

The ball was originally ruled a double, but officials convened and got the call right, ruling the shot hit off a fan and bounced back on the field.

The Sox, who improved to 10-2 in their last 11 chances to avoid postseason elimination, will be looking for their first trip to the World Series since 1986, but they've been in this position before, only to crumble. Last year, they forced a seventh game at Yankee Stadium with a 9-6 win in Game 6, but Pedro Martinez couldn't nail down a three-run lead with five outs remaining, leading to a crushing, 11-inning defeat on Aaron Boone's walk-off homer.

"We remember what a gut-wrenching loss that was, and it's something that will only make us stronger," Kevin Millar said.

The Yankees, meanwhile, will be looking to clinch their 40th AL pennant and return to the World Series to avenge their upset defeat to the Florida Marlins last October.

ABOVE: Curt Schilling fulfilled his wish, silencing the Yankee crowd with seven strong innings in Game 6 of the ALCS at Yankee Stadium. (Matt Stone/Boston Herald)

"The pressure's on them to put us away," Foulke said. "In 20 years, no one's going to remember if Boston lost the series 3-0, 3-1 or 3-2, but everyone will remember how we did it if we go to the World Series."

New York cut it to 4-2 in the eighth on Derek Jeter's RBI single, but the bid to get any closer was cut short when Alex Rodriguez was called out for interference after knocking the ball out of Bronson Arroyo's glove as the relief pitcher applied a tag along the first base line. Angry fans bombarded the field with bottles, baseballs and debris, forcing the umpiring crew to call for the NYPD riot squad to position itself in foul territory.

"If you want to play football, go strap it on for the Green Bay Packers," Millar said of Rodriguez.

"**The pressure's on them to put us away. In 20 years, no one's going to remember if Boston lost the series 3-0, 3-1 or 3-2, but everyone will remember how we did it if we go to the World Series.** "

— Keith Foulke

BELOW: Mark Bellhorn's home run would be the cushion the Red Sox needed to force an unprecedented Game 7. (Matthew West/Boston Herald)

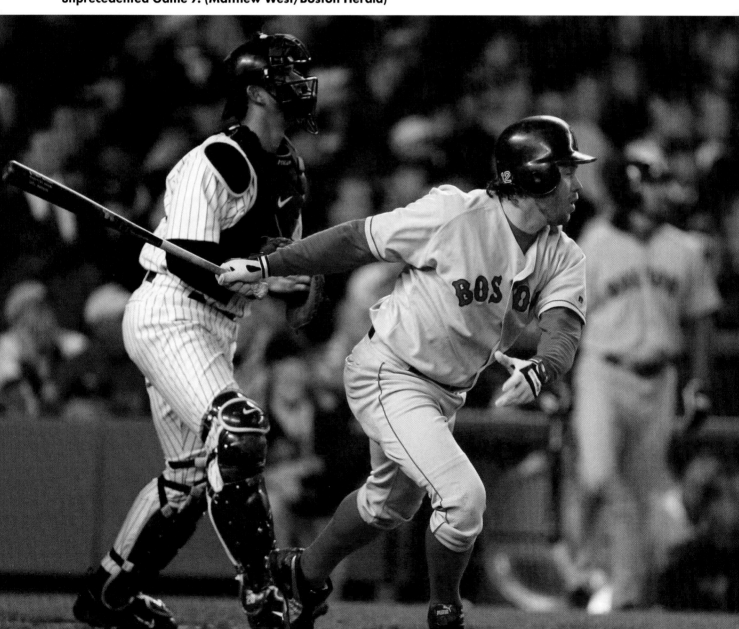

CURT SCHILLING • PITCHER • CURT SCHILLING • PITCHER • CURT SCHILLING • PITCH
CURT SCHILLING • PITCHER • CURT SCHILLING • PITCHER • CURT SCHILLING • PITCH
CURT SCHILLING • PITCHER • CURT SCHILLING • PITCHER • CURT SCHILLING • PITCH
CURT SCHILLING • PITCHER • CURT SCHILLING • PITCHER • CURT SCHILLING • PITCH
CURT SCHILLING • PITCHER • CURT SCHILLING • PITCHER • CURT SCHILLING • PITCH

CURT SCHILLING

BY MICHAEL SILVERMAN

With the aid of fresh stitches in his ankle, prayer in his heart and nasty pitches coming out of his hand, Curt Schilling was able to shut down the Yankees' lineup for seven dominant innings.

He also, almost single-handedly, kept hope alive for the Red Sox.

Without Schilling's effort in the Red Sox' 4-2 Game 6 victory, it is difficult to imagine the Sox playing in Game 7. After crediting his faith in a higher power for giving him "the strength to go out there tonight and compete," Schilling revealed startling details about the state of his dislocated peroneal ankle tendon.

Although he experimented with a high-top cleat to shore up his injury, a last-ditch medical effort made last night's start possible: sutures that stabilized the tendon and allowed Schilling to pitch "normally."

"I couldn't wear the high-tops, they were putting too much pressure on the stitches around the sutured area," Schilling said. "To avoid having [the tendon] popping in and out, they sutured the skin down to something in between the two tendons to keep the tendon out. And it worked."

Schilling said the suturing was done Oct. 18.

"We were going to wait until today, but I felt yesterday that I needed a day to get used to it and so we did it yesterday," Schilling said.

With the tendon stabilized, there was no repetition of Schilling's poor performance in Game 1, when he allowed six runs and six hits in three painful-to-watch innings.

In Game 6 Schilling was able to live his dream of effectively silencing the 56,128 Yankees fans who got to watch him shut down their vaunted sluggers. The infield pop-ups, foul balls and even the deep flies caught by Sox outfielders gave testament to how the Yankees hitters were unable to zone in on Schilling's pitches and make the kind of contact they did in Game 1.

Bernie Williams did succeed in the seventh, launching a ball into the upper deck in right for a one-out solo home run. Other than a Miguel Cairo ground-rule double in the third, no one else inflicted serious damage against Schilling.

Alex Rodriguez and Gary Sheffield led off the fourth with back-to-back singles, the biggest threat of the evening. But Schilling retired the next three batters—Hideki Matsui (foul out to first base) and Bernie Williams and Jorge Posada (both ground outs to first base).

Schilling was at 99 pitches when he walked off the mound after out No. 21. His pitch efficiency was critical to the Red Sox, whose bullpen was decimated from the 12- and 14-inning battles in Games 4 and 5 at Fenway Park the previous two nights. The Red Sox needed just an inning apiece from Bronson Arroyo and Keith Foulke for Schilling's win to be preserved and the Red Sox to live another day.

"My goal was to pitch as normal as I could pitch," Schilling said.

The circumstances were anything but normal, but his pitching was and, because of that, the Red Sox can thank Schilling for living to play another day.

DAMON, SOX
MAKE HISTORY

BY JEFF HORRIGAN, BOSTON HERALD

It didn't take a baseball scholar to interpret the intentions of the New York Yankees when they arranged to have Bucky Dent throw out the ceremonial first pitch before the decisive seventh game of the American League Championship Series at Yankee Stadium.

	1	2	3		4	5	6		7	8	9		R	H	E
Boston	2	4	0		2	0	0		0	1	1		10	13	0
NY Yankees	0	0	1		0	0	0		2	0	0		3	5	1

Boston	AB	R	H	RBI
Damon, CF	6	2	3	6
Bellhorn, 2B	3	1	1	1
Reese, 2B	0	1	0	0
Ramirez, LF	5	1	1	0
Ortiz, DH	4	1	1	2
Varitek, C	5	0	1	0
Nixon, RF	5	1	1	0
Millar, 1B	3	1	1	0
Mientkiewicz, 1B	1	0	1	0
Mueller, 3B	4	1	2	0
Cabrera, SS	2	2	1	1
Totals	38	10	13	10

N.Y. Yankees	AB	R	H	RBI
Jeter, SS	4	0	1	1
Rodriguez, 3B	4	0	0	0
Sheffield, RF	4	0	0	0
Matsui, LF	4	1	2	0
Williams, CF	4	1	1	1
Posada, C	3	0	0	0
Lofton, DH	3	0	1	1
Clark, 1B	2	0	0	0
Olerud, PH-1B	1	0	0	0
Sierra, R., PH	1	0	0	0
Cairo, 2B	2	1	0	0
Totals	32	3	5	3

2B: Matsui, Williams, HR: Ortiz (3), Damon 2 (3), Bellhorn (2). SB: Damon, Cairo , Lofton.
E: Loaiza.

Boston	IP	H	R	ER	BB	SO
Lowe (W, 1-0)	6.0	1	1	1	1	3
Martinez, P	1.0	3	2	2	0	1
Timlin	1.2	1	0	0	1	1
Embree	0.1	0	0	0	0	0

N.Y. Yankees	IP	H	R	ER	BB	SO
Brown (L, 0-1)	1.1	4	5	5	2	1
Vazquez	2.0	2	3	3	5	2
Loaiza	3.0	4	0	0	0	2
Heredia	0.2	0	0	0	0	0
Gordon	1.2	3	2	2	0	0
Rivera	0.1	0	0	0	0	0

HBP: Cairo (by Lowe); T: 3:31; Att: 56,129.

By calling on the former light-hitting shortstop, who sank the Red Sox with an unlikely home run off Mike Torrez in a one-game playoff for the AL East title in 1978, even an idiot could see that the smug Yankees were giving their fans a knowing wink and a reassuring, unspoken message: "Don't worry, they'll blow it again."

In the end, however, the roles were delightfully reversed. Johnny Damon broke out of his ALCS slump by belting two home runs and driving in six runs to send the Sox to a 10-3 victory and saddle the Yankees with the dubious dishonor in Major League Baseball's annals as the biggest chokers of all time.

Just three outs away from sweeping the Sox on Oct. 17 at Fenway Park, the team with the game's highest payroll became the first one in baseball history to take a 3-0 lead and lose a seven-game series. The Sox' incredible recovery from the brink of elimination earned them their first berth in the World Series since 1986.

"Four or five days ago, no one gave us a chance, but here we are, going to the World Series," manager Terry Francona said. "We didn't want to be down, 0-3, but we fought back. We didn't give up, just like we didn't give up in July, when we were treading water there. And we're still not going to give up."

Tim Wakefield is expected to start for Boston in Game 1, when the 100th Fall Classic opens against either Houston or St. Louis at Fenway Park. The Sox, of course, will be looking for their first World Series title since 1918.

The Sox jumped ahead, 2-0, in the first inning on David Ortiz' two-run homer and never let up on the beleaguered New York pitching staff. They out-hit the Yankees, 13-5, and received an outstanding pitching performance from starter Derek Lowe, who allowed only one run on one hit in six innings. Damon, who was 3-for-29 in the first six games of the series, went 3-for-6, while the unbelievably clutch Ortiz was named the series' Most Valuable Player.

"This is a historic event," Lowe said. "Words can't even describe it because it's never been done before. I hope people appreciate what just happened."

Managers Francona and Joe Torre waited until the afternoon to officially name their starting pitchers but cautioned that neither Lowe nor Kevin Brown were being counted upon to work deep into the game.

Few expected, however, that Brown would spit the proverbial bit for the third straight start against the Sox. The right-hander, who lasted

BELOW: Johnny Damon gives the Sox an early lead with a grand slam in the second inning. (Matthew West/Boston Herald)

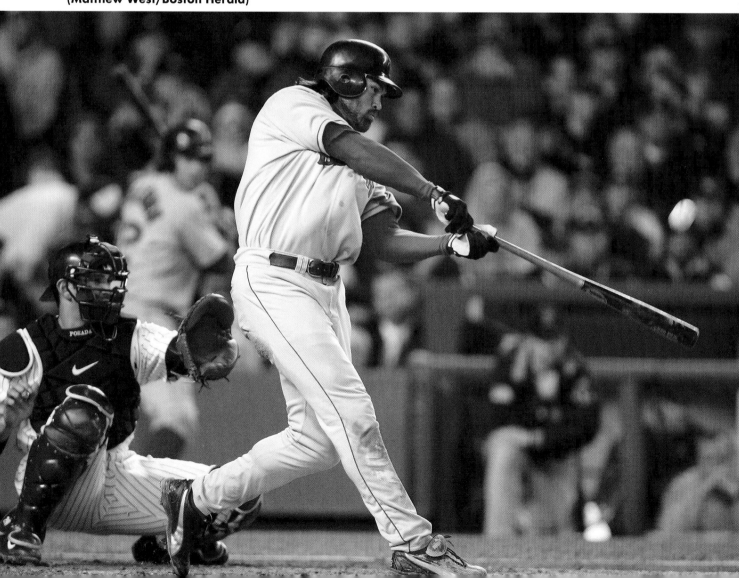

ABOVE: Bill Mueller throws Alex Rodriguez out at first. (Matthew West/Boston Herald)

only 1/3 inning on Sept. 26 and just two innings in Game 3, was knocked out after 1 1/3 innings this time. He once again struggled with his command and had no life on his pitches, leading to five runs allowed on four hits and two walks.

The Sox didn't waste any time jumping on Brown. Damon opened the game by slapping a single to left and stole second but he was thrown out at the plate trying to score on Manny Ramirez' one-out single. The crowd let out a sigh of relief, feeling the Yanks had stemmed the Sox' momentum, but Ortiz turned them into gasps of horror by belting Brown's next pitch into the right field seats.

Torre quickly pulled the plug on Brown, who loaded the bases with one out in the second on a single and a pair of walks, only to see the game slip away on reliever Javier Vazquez' first pitch. Damon pulled it down the right field line, where it landed in the front row for the second grand slam in Sox postseason history.

New York scored a run in the third, but Damon countered by pounding a two-run homer into the top deck in right field to push the Boston lead to 8-1.

"Four or five days ago, no one gave us a chance, but here we are, going to the World Series. We didn't want to be down, 0-3, but we fought back. We didn't give up, just like we didn't give up in July, when we were treading water there. And we're still not going to give up."

—Terry Francona

RIGHT: Jason Varitek jumps into the arms of pitcher Alan Embree after winning Game 7 of the ALCS against the Yankees at Yankee Stadium. (David Goldman/Boston Herald)

SOX TOOT THEIR OWN BELLHORN IN GAME 1

BY JEFF HORRIGAN, BOSTON HERALD

	1 2 3	4 5 6	7 8 9	R	H	E
St. Louis	0 1 1	3 0 2	0 2 0	9	11	1
Boston	4 0 3	0 0 0	2 2 X	11	13	4

St. Louis	AB	R	H	RBI
Renteria, SS	4	1	2	1
Walker, RF	5	1	4	2
Pujols, 1B	3	0	0	0
Rolen, 3B	5	0	0	0
Edmonds, CF	4	2	1	0
Sanders, DH	3	1	0	0
Womack, 2B	1	1	0	0
Anderson, 2B	2	0	1	0
Matheny, C	2	0	1	2
Marquis, PR	0	1	0	0
Molina, C	1	0	0	0
Taguchi, LF	3	1	1	1
Cedeno, PH-LF	2	1	1	0
Totals	**35**	**9**	**11**	**6**

Boston	AB	R	H	RBI
Damon, CF	6	1	2	1
Cabrera, SS	4	2	1	1
Ramirez, LF	5	0	3	2
Ortiz, DH	3	1	2	4
Millar, 1B	5	1	1	0
Mientkiewicz, 1B	0	0	0	0
Nixon, RF	3	0	0	0
Kapler, PH-RF	1	0	0	0
Mueller, 3B	3	1	1	1
Mirabelli, C	3	1	1	0
Varitek, PH-C	2	1	0	0
Bellhorn, 2B	3	3	2	2
Reese, 2B	0	0	0	0
Totals	**38**	**11**	**13**	**11**

2B: Walker 2, Renteria, Anderson, Damon, Millar; HR: Walker (1), Ortiz (1), Bellhorn (1).
E: Renteria, Millar, Arroyo, Ramirez 2; PB: Mirabelli.

St. Louis	IP	H	R	ER	BB	SO
Williams	2.1	8	7	7	3	1
Haren	3.2	2	0	0	3	1
Calero	0.1	1	2	2	2	0
King	0.1	1	0	0	0	0
Eldred	0.1	0	0	0	0	1
Tavarez (L, 0-1)	1.0	1	2	1	0	0

Boston	IP	H	R	ER	BB	SO
Wakefield	3.2	3	5	5	5	2
Arroyo	2.1	4	2	2	0	4
Timlin	1.1	1	1	1	0	0
Embree	0.0	1	1	0	0	0
Foulke (W, 1-0)	1.2	2	0	0	1	3

HBP: Cabrera (by Williams), Pujols (by Wakefield); T: 4:00; Att: 35,035.

When the Red Sox were paired up with the St. Louis Cardinals in the 100th World Series, there was no way that Johnny Pesky could avoid being an integral part of the story line.

The 85-year-old Boston legend was vilified for allegedly holding the ball too long on a relay throw in Game 7 of the 1946 World Series, and when the Sox committed four errors, leading to blown leads of 7-2 and 9-7, it appeared that they would pine for the day that anyone would hold the ball.

In the end, however, it was the Pesky Pole that drew the focus away from the sloppy play. Mark Bellhorn belted a tie-breaking, two-run home run off the right field foul pole off Julian Tavarez with one out in the bottom of the eighth inning to send the Sox to an 11-9 victory and move them to within three wins of their first championship in 86 years.

A pair of errors by left fielder Manny Ramirez in the top of the eighth inning allowed St. Louis to score two runs, erasing Boston's 9-7 lead, but Bellhorn broke the deadlock by lining a shot off the top of the foul pole named in former light-hitting infielder Pesky's honor because it is the shortest distance (302 feet) to a homer at Fenway.

"Every little boy always thinks about playing in the World Series and winning the game," Bellhorn said. "I know I did, but I'm not here to try to be a hero, just to win four games."

It marked the second straight game that the second baseman homered off the right field foul pole. Bellhorn also hit one off the pole at Yankee Stadium in the eighth inning of the pennant-clinching win.

"That home run was a big relief," Ramirez said. "That's why you have teammates, to pick you up."

BELOW: Sox Mark Bellhorn hits the game-winning home run in the eighth inning to put the Sox up 11-9 in Game 1 of the World Series. (Matthew West/Boston Herald)

The Sox tied the 1903 franchise record for most runs scored in a World Series game, and they needed virtually every one of them.

Run-scoring singles by Ramirez and David Ortiz in the seventh inning broke a 7-7 tie, but the advantage quickly slipped through the Sox' hands in the top of the eighth. With two on and one out, Edgar Renteria bounced a single through the left side of the infield that Ramirez overran, neglecting to pick up cleanly. Pinch runner Jason Marquis scored, cutting the lead to 9-8.

Larry Walker (4-for-5) followed with a flare to shallow left that Ramirez should have caught, only to catch his cleat on the turf as he slid under the ball, resulting in him popping up and dropping it. Roger Cedeno scored the tying run, but the Sox were unfazed.

"I just rushed," Ramirez said. "I shouldn't have dove for the ball. . . . It just goes to show that it's not over until the last out because anything can happen."

Jason Varitek reached on an error with one out in the bottom of the inning, and

ABOVE: Sox Manny Ramirez celebrates at first base after he hits an RBI single that scores the go-ahead run in the seventh inning. (Matthew West/Boston Herald)

Bellhorn took advantage by following with a blast off the pole.

Keith Foulke, who was charged with an unjust blown save in the top of the eighth, allowed a one-out double to Marlon Anderson in the ninth but retired the next two, striking out Cedeno to end the game and earn the win.

Ortiz' four RBIs tied a Sox record for a World Series game that was established by Carl Yastrzemski against the Cardinals in Game 2 of the 1967 series. The slugger already has 19 RBIs in the current postseason, tying the record shared by Sandy Alomar Jr. (1997) and Scott Spiezio (2002).

"We didn't play that well," Ortiz said. "Errors cost us five or six runs, and I hope that changes tomorrow."

ABOVE: Sox Manny Ramirez misses a hit by Larry Walker that allowed the Cardinals to get two runs and tie the score in the eighth inning. (Matt Stone/Boston Herald)

OPPOSITE: Sox Orlando Cabrera gets hit by a pitch from Woody Williams in the first inning. (Matt Stone/Boston Herald)

" Every little boy always thinks about playing in the World Series and winning the game. I know I did, but I'm not here to try to be a hero, just to win four games."

—Mark Bellhorn

SOX STITCH TOGETHER 2-0 SERIES LEAD VS. CARDINALS

BY JEFF HORRIGAN, BOSTON HERALD

Recent history has proved that it is absolutely foolish to start celebrating after taking a 2-0 lead in a best-of-seven series. But the Red Sox and their fervent, faithful followers have to feel awfully good about capturing their first World Series championship in 86 years.

Responding remarkably well to an experimental procedure on his right ankle for the second consecutive start, Curt Schilling pitched six strong innings to lead the Sox to a 6-2 victory over the St. Louis Cardinals in Game 2 of the 100th World Series at Fenway Park.

Schilling allowed only an unearned run on four hits, while striking out four batters, and became the first hurler in history to win World Series games for three different teams. The right-hander, who had his skin sutured to deep tissue to hold a dislocated tendon in place, was also victorious for Philadelphia (1993) and Arizona (2001).

St. Louis scored its only run against Schilling on the second of third baseman Bill Mueller's three errors.

The Sox became the 49th team to jump out to a 2-0 lead in the World Series. Thirty-seven of the preceding 48 (77.1 percent) teams went on to win the title. In addition, each of the last nine home teams to win the first two games has gone on to win the World Series.

	1	2	3	4	5	6	7	8	9	R	H	E
St. Louis	0	0	0	1	0	0	0	1	0	2	5	0
Boston	2	0	0	2	0	2	0	0	X	6	8	4

St. Louis		AB		R		H		RBI
Renteria, SS		3		1		0		0
Walker, RF		4		0		0		0
Pujols, 1B		4		1		3		0
Rolen, 3B		3		0		0		1
Edmonds, CF		4		0		0		0
Sanders, LF		3		0		0		0
Womack, 2B		4		0		1		0
Matheny, C		4		0		1		0
Anderson, DH		2		0		0		0
Taguchi, PH-DH		1		0		0		0
Totals		32		2		5		1

Boston		AB		R		H		RBI
Damon, CF		5		1		1		0
Cabrera, SS		4		0		1		2
Ramirez, LF		4		1		1		0
Kapler, LF		0		0		0		0
Ortiz, DH		3		1		0		0
Varitek, C		3		0		1		2
Millar, 1B		1		1		0		0
Mientkiewicz, PR-1B		0		0		0		0
Nixon, RF		4		1		1		0
Mueller, 3B		3		1		2		0
Bellhorn, 2B		3		0		1		2
Reese, 2B		1		0		0		0
Totals		31		6		8		6

2B: Pujols 2, Mueller, Bellhorn; 3B: Varitek; E: Mueller 3, Bellhorn.

St. Louis	IP	H	R	ER	BB	SO
Morris (L, 0-1)	4.1	4	4	4	4	3
Eldred	1.1	4	2	2	0	1
King	0.1	0	0	0	0	1
Marquis	1.0	0	0	0	2	0
Reyes	1.0	0	0	0	0	0

Boston	IP	H	R	ER	BB	SO
Schilling (W, 1-0)	6.0	4	1	0	1	4
Embree	1.0	0	0	0	0	3
Timlin	0.2	1	1	1	1	0
Foulke	1.1	0	0	0	0	2

HBP: Millar (by Morris), Varitek (by Eldred); T: 3:20; Att: 35,001.

ABOVE: Sox second baseman Mark Bellhorn gets Mike Matheny out for the first out of a double play to end the fifth inning. (Matthew West/Boston Herald)

The Sox have gone up 2-0 in two other Fall Classics. They went on to defeat Brooklyn in 1916 but let a title slip away to the New York Mets in 1986.

"We've got to keep playing hard because you've got to win four games to be a champ," left fielder Manny Ramirez said. "We're close but we're still not there yet."

Jason Varitek, Mark Bellhorn and Orlando Cabrera knocked in two runs apiece, and the Sox overcame four errors for the second consecutive night to win their sixth consecutive postseason game.

"So far, we've been able to carry [the momentum from the ALCS] over to this series," said reliever Alan Embree, who struck out all three batters he faced in the seventh. "We feed off positive energy. We are not going to fall into

the trap after winning the first two. You saw what happened with the Yankees."

The series now shifts to St. Louis, where the teams resume play at Busch Stadium after an off day.

"We haven't done anything yet," first baseman Kevin Millar said. "They're a tough ballclub and we're going to a tough ballpark to play in."

For the second straight night, a St. Louis starting pitcher failed to last five innings, forcing the bullpen to work overtime. Woody Williams was hammered for seven runs in only 2 1/3 innings in Game 1; Matt Morris was knocked out of Game 2 after allowing four runs on four hits and four walks in 4 1/3 innings.

Morris only had himself to blame for allowing the Sox to pull out to a 2-0 first-inning lead. The right-hander issued consecutive, two-out

BELOW: Sox third baseman Bill Mueller catches a line drive for an unassisted double play in the second inning. (Matthew West/Boston Herald)

ABOVE: Sox David Ortiz argues that his fifth-inning long ball was a home run after it was ruled foul by the umpires. (Matthew West/Boston Herald)

walks to Ramirez and David Ortiz before Varitek made him pay by lining a two-run triple off the side wall of the Red Sox' bullpen in the center field triangle.

The Cardinals cut the lead to 2-1 with the unearned run in the fourth, but the Red Sox made sure momentum didn't shift. The Sox responded with a pair of runs in the bottom half of the inning to push the lead to 4-1. With two on and two out, Bellhorn blasted a double off the base of the center field wall, allowing Millar and Mueller to score.

The lead jumped to 6-1 in the sixth inning on Cabrera's two-run, two-out single off the Green Monster against reliever Cal Eldred.

"If you get the two-out hits and you can stop the two-out hit, that's one of those formulas that will win a lot of games for you," lamented Cardinals manager Tony La Russa.

St. Louis closed out the scoring in the eighth on Scott Rolen's sacrifice fly off reliever Mike Timlin.

ABOVE: Sox hurler Curt Schilling takes a break on the mound during the fifth inning. Schilling, who became the first pitcher to win games for three different teams, allowed one unearned run on four hits. (Matt Stone/Boston Herald)

" So far, we've been able to carry [the momentum from the ALCS] over to this series. We feed off positive energy. We are not going to fall into the trap after winning the first two. You saw what happened with the Yankees. "

—Alan Embree

BELOW: Sox closer Keith Foulke pumps his fist after clinching the 6-2 Sox win in Game 2. (Matthew West/Boston Herald)

WAKE UP THE BABE

BY JEFF HORRIGAN, BOSTON HERALD

	1 2 3	4 5 6	7 8 9	R	H	E
Boston	1 0 0	1 2 0	0 0 0	4	9	0
St. Louis	0 0 0	0 0 0	0 0 1	1	4	0

Boston	AB	R	H	RBI
Damon, CF	5	1	1	0
Cabrera, SS	4	1	2	0
Ramirez, LF	4	1	2	2
Ortiz, 1B	4	0	1	0
Mientkiewicz, 1B	0	0	0	0
Varitek, C	3	0	0	0
Mueller, 3B	4	1	2	1
Nixon, RF	3	0	1	1
Kapler, PH-RF	1	0	0	0
Bellhorn, 2B	3	0	0	0
Reese, 2B	0	0	0	0
Martinez, P., P	2	0	0	0
Millar, PH	1	0	0	0
Timlin, P	0	0	0	0
Foulke, P	0	0	0	0
Totals	34	4	9	4

St. Louis	AB	R	H	RBI
Renteria, SS	4	0	1	0
Walker, RF	3	1	1	1
Pujols, 1B	4	0	1	0
Rolen, 3B	3	0	0	0
Edmonds, CF	3	0	0	0
Sanders, LF	3	0	0	0
Womack, 2B	3	0	0	0
Matheny, C	2	0	0	0
Cedeno, PH	1	0	0	0
Tavarez, P	0	0	0	0
Suppan, P	1	0	1	0
Reyes, P	0	0	0	0
Anderson, PH	1	0	0	0
Calero, P	0	0	0	0
King, P	0	0	0	0
Mabry, PH	1	0	0	0
Molina, C	0	0	0	0
Totals	29	1	4	1

2B: Mueller, Damon, Cabrera, Renteria. HR: Ramirez (1), Walker (2).

Boston	IP	H	R	ER	BB	SO
Martinez, P (W, 1-0)	7.0	3	0	0	2	6
Timlin	1.0	0	0	0	0	0
Foulke	1.0	1	1	1	0	2

St. Louis	IP	H	R	ER	BB	SO
Suppan (L, 0-1)	4.2	8	4	4	1	4
Reyes	0.1	0	0	0	0	0
Calero	1.0	1	0	0	2	0
King	2.0	0	0	0	1	0
Tavarez	1.0	0	0	0	0	1

HBP: Bellhorn (by Suppan); T: 2:58; Att: 52,015.

One more win.

That is all it is going to take now for the Red Sox to exorcise the demons of 86 years and allow the tormented souls of generations of departed New Englanders to finally rest in peace by finishing off the St. Louis Cardinals in the 100th World Series.

Pedro Martinez made the most of his long-awaited opportunity to appear in the Fall Classic, pitching seven scoreless innings to lead the Sox to a 4-1 victory at Busch Stadium and a commanding three games to none lead in the best-of-seven series.

Martinez allowed only three hits, struck out six and held the Cardinals hitless in six at-bats with runners in scoring position. The three-time Cy Young Award winner was sluggish at the outset, but St. Louis helped him find his rhythm by running into deflating double plays in the first and third innings. Martinez

OPPOSITE: Pedro Martinez and the Sox escape a bases-loaded jam in the first when Jason Varitek tags out the Cardinals' Larry Walker for the third out. (David Goldman/Boston Herald)

finished up by retiring the final 14 batters he faced.

"That could be one of the happiest moments I've ever had for somebody," catcher Jason Varitek said. "As much scrutiny as he's had sometimes, with as great a career as he's had, that was phenomenal."

The effort helped the Sox become the 21st team to surge to a 3-0 lead in World Series history. All 20 predecessors went on to win the title,

including 17 by sweeps. Each of the last five teams to take a 3-0 lead has won the championship in four games. St. Louis has not held a lead in any game this series.

"We're up, 3-0, and that's a good way to start a series, but we're not done," Johnny Damon said. "With what we did [to the New York Yankees] last week, we know not to be satisfied yet."

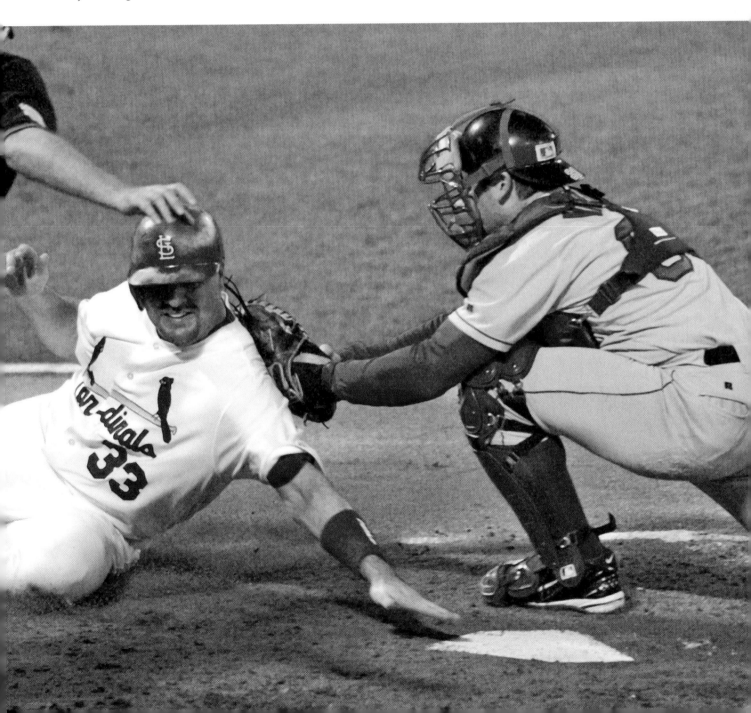

ABOVE: Sox hurler Pedro Martinez did everything right in Game 3 against the Cardinals. He pitched seven scoreless innings and retired the final 14 batters he faced. (Stuart Cahill/Boston Herald)

" That could be one of the happiest moments I've ever had for somebody. As much scrutiny as he's had sometimes, with as great a career as he's had, that was phenomenal."

—Jason Varitek on Pedro Martinez

ABOVE: All-day rain before Game 3 created a swampy right field, causing Trot Nixon to fall down on a hit by Edgar Renteria at Busch Stadium. (Matt Stone/Boston Herald)

The Sox extended their winning streak to seven games, which matches the longest ever in the postseason (shared by the 1998 Yankees, 1995 Atlanta Braves and 1976 Cincinnati Reds). No team has ever won eight straight postseason games.

"We're not comfortable yet because we've seen the other side of this," said reliever Mike Timlin.

The Sox pounded Cardinals starter Jeff Suppan for four runs on eight hits in only 4 2/3 innings, and the ex-Red Sox hurler compound-

ABOVE: Manny Ramirez staked the Sox to an early 1-0 lead with a first-inning home run. (Matthew West/Boston Herald)

ed his own problems by making an incredibly stupid baserunning mistake in the third inning that ran his team out of a potential rally.

Suppan's struggles were immediate. With two outs in the first inning, Manny Ramirez clobbered a 91 mph fastball deep into the left field seats for his first home run of the Series.

St. Louis native Bill Mueller made it 2-0 in the fourth inning when he lined a two-out double to the left-center field gap and scored when Trot Nixon followed with a single to right.

The Sox knocked out Suppan in the fifth by scoring two more runs. Damon lined a leadoff

double over the head of right fielder Larry Walker and scored on successive singles by Orlando Cabrera and Ramirez (RBI). Mueller's two-out single to right made it 4-0 and ended Suppan's evening.

The Cardinals had their shot at Martinez early but failed. An infield single and two walks loaded the bases with one out in the first inning, but Walker tried to score from third base on Jim Edmonds' fly to mid-left field and was thrown out at the plate by Ramirez' perfect, one-hop throw to Varitek.

In the third, Suppan reached safely on a leadoff dribbler down the third base line and moved to third on Edgar Renteria's double. Walker followed with a grounder to second baseman Mark Bellhorn, who threw to first for the out, but Suppan hesitated and stopped less than halfway to the plate, even though the Sox had the infield back. First baseman David Ortiz'

eyes widened, seemingly in disbelief that Suppan had really not scored, and he fired over to third baseman Mueller, who applied the tag to the retreating runner.

"David made a beautiful throw to third," Varitek said. "Had he not put the ball where he did, Suppan would have been safe."

BELOW: Bill Mueller tags out Jeff Suppan at third for a double play in the third. (Matthew West/Boston Herald)

RED SOX 86
THE CURSE

BY JEFF HORRIGAN, BOSTON HERALD

	1	2	3	4	5	6	7	8	9	R	H	E
Boston	1	0	2	0	0	0	0	0	0	3	9	0
St. Louis	0	0	0	0	0	0	0	0	0	0	4	0

Boston	AB	R	H	RBI
Damon, CF	5	1	2	1
Cabrera, SS	5	0	0	0
Ramirez, LF	4	0	1	0
Ortiz, 1B	3	1	1	0
Mientkiewicz, 1B	1	0	0	0
Varitek, C	5	1	1	0
Mueller, 3B	4	0	1	0
Nixon, RF	4	0	3	2
Kapler, PR-RF	0	0	0	0
Bellhorn, 2B	1	0	0	0
Reese, PR-2B	0	0	0	0
Lowe, P	2	0	0	0
Millar, PH	1	0	0	0
Arroyo, P	0	0	0	0
Embree, P	0	0	0	0
Foulke, P	0	0	0	0
Totals	**35**	**3**	**9**	**3**

St. Louis	AB	R	H	RBI
Womack, 2B	3	0	1	0
Luna, PH-2B	1	0	0	0
Walker, RF	2	0	0	0
Pujols, 1B	4	0	1	0
Rolen, 3B	4	0	0	0
Edmonds, CF	4	0	0	0
Renteria, SS	4	0	2	0
Mabry, LF	3	0	0	0
Isringhausen, P	0	0	0	0
Molina, C	2	0	0	0
Cedeno, PH	1	0	0	0
Matheny, C	0	0	0	0
Marquis, P	1	0	0	0
Anderson, PH	1	0	0	0
Haren, P	0	0	0	0
Sanders, LF	0	0	0	0
Totals	**30**	**0**	**4**	**0**

2B: Nixon 3, Ortiz, Renteria; 3B: Damon; HR: Damon (1); SB: Sanders.

Boston	IP	H	R	ER	BB	SO
Lowe (W, 1-0)	7.0	3	0	0	1	4
Arroyo	0.1	0	0	0	1	0
Embree	0.2	0	0	0	0	1
Foulke (S, 1)	1.0	1	0	0	0	1

St. Louis	IP	H	R	ER	BB	SO
Marquis (L, 0-1)	6.0	6	3	3	5	4
Haren	1.0	2	0	0	0	1
Isringhausen	2.0	1	0	0	1	2

WP: Lowe; T: 3:14; Att: 52,037.

The sighs of relief, gasps of disbelief and uncontrollable sobs of joy emanating from halfway across the country seemed to reverberate between the mighty metallic spans of the adjacent Gateway Arch.

As the Red Sox stormed out of the visitors' dugout at Busch Stadium to celebrate a 3-0 victory that completed a stunning, four-game sweep of the St. Louis Cardinals, the din of the outpouring of emotion from New England was almost audible through the on-field shouts of jubilation.

Generations of Sox fans went to their graves having never experienced a World Series championship, but after an 86-year wait, the descendants of the unfulfilled exulted for family lines. After all, with a Calvinist way of thinking so deeply engrained in the region's collective psyche, few who watched Derek Lowe master the National League champions for seven shutout innings could believe what they had witnessed. When they awoke this morning, however, a major part of their lives had changed forever.

OPPOSITE: Johnny Damon homers on the fourth pitch of Game 4, giving the Red Sox an early lead. (Matt Stone/Boston Herald)

"So many people can die happy now," general manager Theo Epstein said. "But a whole lot more can live happy. . . . I hope they're getting that '2000!' chant ready for the Yankees in Boston next year."

Just three outs away from being swept by the New York Yankees in the American League Championship Series 10 days earlier, the Sox accomplished the impossible and strung together an eight-game winning streak—the longest ever in a single postseason—to claim the franchise's first World Series title since 1918.

Up above, beyond a thick Midwestern overcast, the first lunar eclipse ever to take place during a World Series methodically passed through its stages, making our fathers and grandfathers prophetic. They were the ones, after all, who professed that the stars would have to be aligned just right for the Sox to win another title.

"Someone said this is the biggest thing to happen in New England since the Revolution," owner John Henry said. "I don't know about that but I know there is an overwhelming sense of joy and relief."

Unthinkable collapses and tragedies over the past 8 1/2 decades made the names Buckner, Galehouse, Boone and Dent just as identifiable with Sox history as stars Foxx, Cronin, Williams, Yastrzemski and Rice, each of whom never experienced the feeling of winning the World Series.

"It's going to be a boring winter in Boston," Alan Embree said. "Let's not wait 86 years again, OK?"

The Sox became the fourth team in history never to trail during the World Series, joining the 1963 Dodgers, 1966 Orioles and 1989 A's.

"We beat the best in the American League, and we beat the best in the National League," shortstop Orlando Cabrera said. "Now there is no one who can say we are not the best."

Lowe, who was demoted from the starting rotation at the beginning of the playoffs, ended up winning the clinching games in each of the three postseason rounds. After limiting the Yankees to one hit in six innings on two days' rest exactly one week earlier, he allowed only three hits and a walk this time. Lowe frustrated the Sox with his inconsistency during the sea-

BELOW: Manny Ramirez is tagged out at the plate in the third inning. (Matthew West/Boston Herald)

ABOVE: Derek Lowe pitched seven shutout innings as the Sox completed the four-game sweep. (Tara Bricking/Boston Herald)

son, but he went 3-0 with a 1.86 ERA during the postseason.

Johnny Damon opened the game by smashing Jason Marquis' 2-and-1 fastball over the right field fence and into the Cardinals' bullpen to become the 17th player in World Series history to open a game with a home run.

The Sox made it 3-0 in the third inning when Trot Nixon pounded Marquis' 3-and-0 fastball off the right field wall with the bases loaded, scoring David Ortiz and Jason Varitek. Lowe and relievers Embree, Bronson Arroyo and Keith Foulke made it stand.

"Like everyone else, I live and die with every pitch of this team," Nixon said. "I know how much this means to the city of Boston. I'm so happy for everyone there."

ABOVE: Keith Foulke celebrates after he threw out Edgar Renteria at first to win the Sox' first World Series title in 86 years. (Stuart Cahill/Boston Herald)

OPPOSITE: The Sox celebrate their world championship. (Tara Bricking/Boston Herald)

MOST VALUABLE PLAYER • MVP • MOST VALUABLE PLAYER • MVP • MOST VALUA
AYER • MVP • MOST VALUABLE PLAYER • MVP • MOST VALUABLE PLAYER • MV
OST VALUABLE PLAYER • MVP • MOST VALUABLE PLAYER • MVP • MOST VALUAI
AYER • MVP • MOST VALUABLE PLAYER • MVP • MOST VALUABLE PLAYER • MV
OST VALUABLE PLAYER • MVP • MOST VALUABLE PLAYER • MVP • MOST VALUAI

MANNY RAMIREZ

BY STEPHEN HARRIS

Looking as happy as any human being has a right to be, Manny Ramirez was in enemy territory in the bowels of Busch Stadium, strolling hand-in-hand with his wife, Juliana, past the entrance to the Cardinals' clubhouse.

Ramirez, oblivious to the stares of various Cardinals' wives and friends who were dealing with a crushing defeat, stopped and gave his wife a kiss.

"Hey, we did it man, we broke the curse," he said.

Ramirez just had been named Most Valuable Player of the 100th World Series, captured by his Red Sox in a four-game sweep of the vaunted Cardinals that was capped by a 3-0 shutout.

Ramirez hit .412 for the Series, with seven hits in 17 at-bats, putting an exclamation point on a remarkable 10-month odyssey that started with the Sox placing the high-priced slugger on waivers during the offseason.

"I went through a lot of drama in the winter, but I kept my mind positive," he said. "I told my wife before the season started, 'Hey baby, this is going to be the year.' Before we went to spring training I told my wife, 'Hey, I'm going to be the MVP of something,' and I did it. I took this thing to the World Series. Me, David [Ortiz] and the rest of the guys, we all did our part and we did it. We're No. 1."

Ramirez engraved his name even deeper into baseball's record books in October. He had at least one base hit in each of the Sox' 13 post-season games, finishing 21-for-60 (.350) with two home runs and 11 RBIs. He now has a 17-game postseason hitting streak, matching the major league record shared by Yankees Derek Jeter and Hank Bauer.

Ramirez vowed after Game 4 that the Sox will be back in the playoffs next year, giving him a chance to take sole possession of the mark.

"Next year?" he said in the champagne-soaked Red Sox clubhouse. "I guess we have to go and do it again."

Ramirez finally has achieved one of his two career goals.

"I have two things in my mind I wanted to accomplish before I'm finished with this game," he said. "First was to get the ring. Second was to get to the Hall of Fame. That's two things that no one can take away from you."

Ramirez said he and his teammates were determined not to let the Series slip even slightly out of their grasp, a lesson they learned from their dramatic ALCS win against New York.

"I think we learned a lot when we played the Yankees, because we lost the first three games and came back," he said. "Yesterday I was talking to the guys and I said, `Hey, let's go, we can't let these guys breathe.'"

Ramirez was one of the poster boys for the team's loose, fun-loving attitude the entire season.

"The game is supposed to be fun, and when you go out with that mentality, that your teammates trust you and they're going to pick you up when you do things wrong, the game becomes more easy for you," he said. "We're just a bunch of idiots. We go out there and have fun. We don't think. We eliminate thinking. We have fun."

Matt Stone/Boston Her

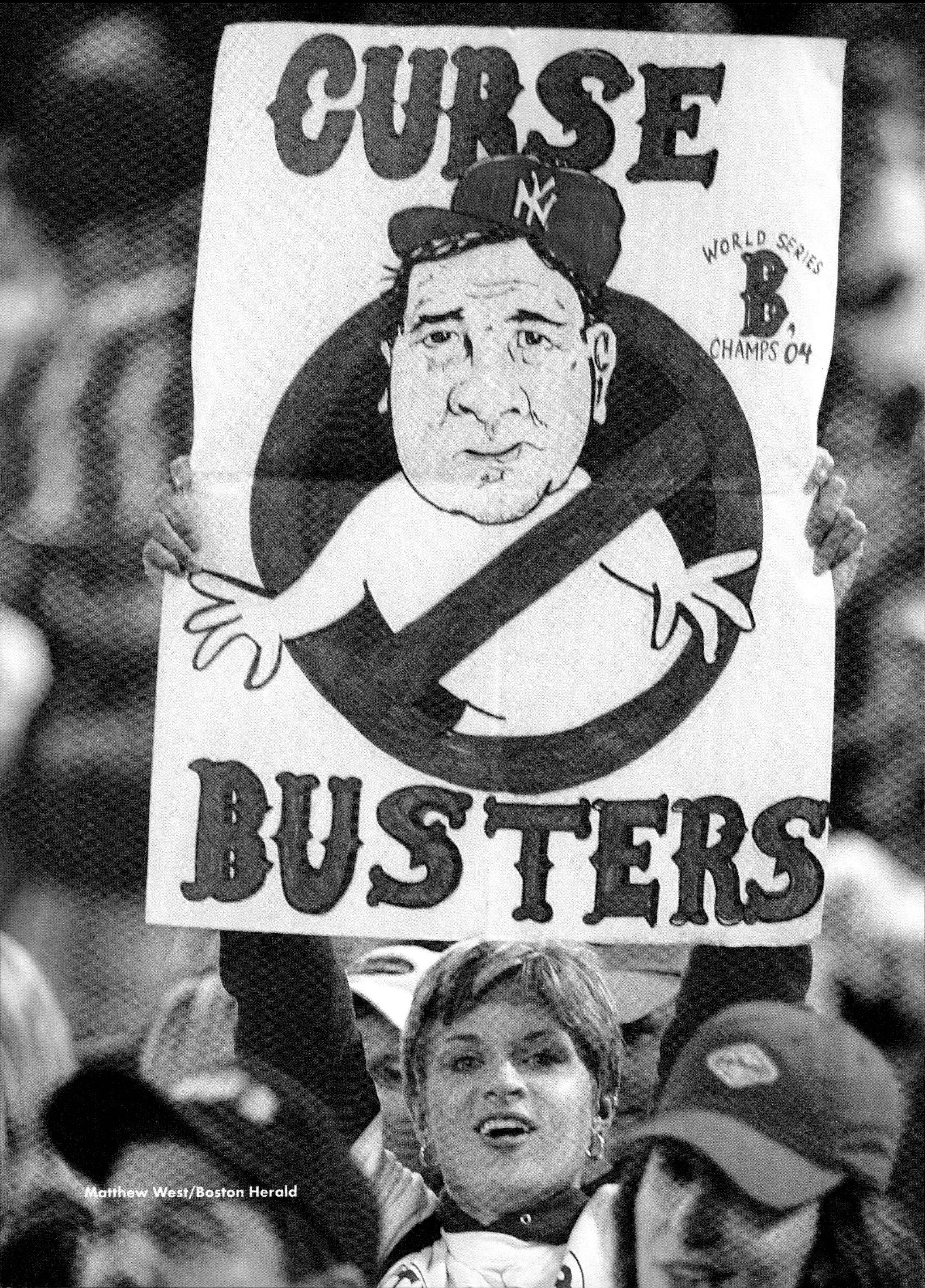

Matthew West/Boston Herald

2004 REGULAR SEASON STATISTICS

Batting

NAME	G	AB	R	H	2B	3B	HR	RBI	TB	BB	SO	SB	CS	OBP	SLG	AVG
Nomar Garciaparra	38	156	24	50	7	3	5	21	78	8	16	2	0	.367	.500	.321
Trot Nixon	48	149	24	47	9	1	6	23	76	15	24	0	0	.377	.510	.315
Manny Ramirez	152	568	108	175	44	0	43	130	348	82	124	2	4	.397	.613	.308
Johnny Damon	150	621	123	189	35	6	20	94	296	76	71	19	8	.380	.477	.304
David Ortiz	150	582	94	175	47	3	41	139	351	75	133	0	0	.380	.603	.301
Adam Hyzdu	17	10	3	3	2	0	1	2	8	1	2	0	0	.364	.800	.300
Kevin Millar	150	508	74	151	36	0	18	74	241	57	91	1	1	.383	.474	.297
Jason Varitek	137	463	67	137	30	1	18	73	223	62	126	10	3	.390	.482	.296
Orlando Cabrera	58	228	33	67	19	1	6	31	106	11	23	4	1	.320	.465	.294
Bill Mueller	110	399	75	113	27	1	12	57	178	51	56	2	2	.365	.446	.283
Doug Mirabelli	59	160	27	45	12	0	9	32	84	19	46	0	0	.368	.525	.281
Ricky Gutierrez	21	40	6	11	1	0	0	3	12	2	6	1	0	.310	.300	.275
Gabe Kapler	136	290	51	79	14	1	6	33	113	15	49	5	4	.311	.390	.272
Mark Bellhorn	138	523	93	138	37	3	17	82	232	88	177	6	1	.373	.444	.264
Kevin Youkilis	72	208	38	54	11	0	7	35	86	33	45	0	1	.367	.413	.260
David McCarty	91	151	24	39	8	1	4	17	61	14	40	1	0	.327	.404	.258
Dave Roberts	45	86	19	22	10	0	2	14	38	10	17	5	2	.330	.442	.256
Derrick Lowe	2	4	0	1	1	0	0	1	2	0	1	0	0	.250	.500	.250
Earl Snyder	1	4	0	1	0	0	0	0	1	0	1	0	0	.250	.250	.250
Doug Mientkiewicz	127	391	47	93	24	1	6	35	137	48	56	2	3	.326	.350	.238
Brian Daubach	30	75	9	17	8	0	2	8	31	10	21	0	0	.326	.413	.227
Pokey Reese	96	244	32	54	7	2	3	29	74	17	60	6	2	.271	.303	.221
Ellis Burks	11	33	6	6	0	0	1	1	9	3	8	2	0	.270	.273	.182
Andy Dominique	7	11	0	2	0	0	0	1	2	0	3	0	0	.182	.182	.182
Cesar Crespo	52	79	6	13	2	1	0	2	17	0	20	2	0	.165	.215	.165
Curt Schilling	2	7	0	1	0	0	0	0	1	0	2	0	0	.143	.143	.143
Bronson Arroyo	3	6	0	0	0	0	0	0	0	0	5	0	0	.000	.000	.000
Sandy Martinez	4	6	0	0	0	0	0	0	0	0	3	0	0	.000	.000	.000
Pedro Martinez	1	2	0	0	0	0	0	0	0	0	1	0	0	.000	.000	.000
Tim Wakefield	1	2	0	0	0	0	0	0	0	0	1	0	0	.000	.000	.000

Pitching

PLAYER	W	L	ERA	G	SV	IP	H	R	ER	BB	SO
Frank Castillo	0	0	0.00	2	0	1	1	0	0	1	0
Phil Seibel	0	0	0.00	2	0	3.2	0	0	0	5	1
Scott Williamson	0	1	1.26	28	1	28.2	11	6	4	18	28
Keith Foulke	5	3	2.17	72	32	83	63	22	20	15	79
David McCarty	0	0	2.45	3	0	3.2	2	1	1	1	4
Curt Schilling	21	6	3.26	32	0	226.2	206	84	82	35	203
Ramiro Mendoza	2	1	3.52	27	0	30.2	25	12	12	7	13
Pedro Martinez	16	9	3.90	33	0	217	193	99	94	61	227
Bronson Arroyo	10	9	4.03	32	0	178.2	171	99	80	47	142
Alan Embree	2	2	4.13	71	0	52.1	49	28	24	11	37
Mike Timlin	5	4	4.13	76	1	76.1	75	35	35	19	56
Lenny DiNardo	0	0	4.23	22	0	27.2	34	17	13	12	21
Mike Malaska	1	1	4.50	19	0	20	21	11	10	12	12
Mike Myers	5	1	4.64	75	0	42.2	45	22	22	23	32
Terry Adams	6	4	4.76	61	3	70	84	39	37	28	56
Tim Wakefield	12	10	4.87	32	0	188.1	197	121	102	63	116
Curtis Leskanic	3	5	5.19	51	4	43.1	47	27	25	30	37
Bobby Jones	0	1	5.40	3	0	3.1	3	2	2	8	3
Derrick Lowe	14	12	5.42	33	0	182.2	224	138	110	71	105
Jamie Brown	0	0	5.87	4	0	7.2	15	7	5	4	6
Jimmy Anderson	0	0	6.00	5	0	6	10	4	4	3	3
Byung-Hyun Kim	2	1	6.23	7	0	17.1	17	15	12	7	6
Anastacio Martinez	2	1	8.44	11	0	10.2	13	10	10	6	5
Abe Alvarez	0	1	9.00	1	0	5	8	5	5	5	2
Pedro Astacio	0	0	10.38	5	0	8.2	13	10	10	5	6
Joe Nelson	0	0	16.87	3	0	2.2	4	5	5	3	5

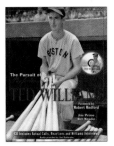

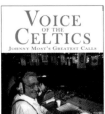